Matterhorn

Steffen Kjaer

ANIARA

Aniara 2024

Translation by Aniara

www.aniara.one

info@aniara.one

Original title (Danish): Matterhorn: Verdens farligste bjerg

ISBN: 978-91-89954-53-3

Contents

Climb if you will, but remember that courage and strength are naught without prudence and that a momentary negligence may destroy the happiness of a lifetime. Do nothing in haste; look well to each step; and from the beginning think what may be the end.

Edward Whymper

Preface

Spectacular! I really cannot think of a word that describes the Matterhorn better. No other mountain in the world has been subject to more attention and fascination than the perfectly shaped Matterhorn since the dramatic first ascent in 1865. Since that day, the drama and the myth have created a unique interest in this mountain, which has probably caused more deaths than any other mountain in the world.

For Brian Jorgensen and I, the decision to attempt to climb the Matterhorn was made with equal measures of fright and admiration. Looking back on our climb, we have both learnt that fascination and horrifying events often go hand in hand.

I am well aware that around the world there are mountains which, technically, are much more difficult to climb than the Matterhorn via the Hörnli Ridge. This book is not written to compare our endeavors with those of others. Rather, I have aimed to tell the story of a mountain that is so spectacular that any mountaineer has got to have it on his or her tick list. Anyway, it was on our list, and so we decided to pursue our dream...

Warning

This is not a guide book, and it is in no way intended as a guide for other climbers. Places and routes are described from my own experiences and will most likely be experienced differently by any other. In the same way, techniques and use of equipment were chosen and used in very specific situations where others may have chosen differently.

Any type of climbing and mountaineering is dangerous. The dangers are everywhere and may very well result in serious injury or death.

The mountains mentioned in this book have all claimed their victims, and nothing indicates that this is going to change in the future. Climbing and mountaineering are dangerous pastimes, and they demand mental and physical fitness, solid background knowledge and a range of skills and equipment to minimize the risks.

To the inexperienced, it may prove hard to determine which knowledge or skills and equipment are necessary to climb a given route or mountain. I therefore recommend that anyone who wants to try his or her hand at mountaineering should participate in approved courses with certified instructors.

Introduction

'Although it is terrifyingly huge, I'm so fascinated by this mountain', said Brian, when we met one evening in March to plan for the coming summer's climbs. His words were embodied by my thoughts. There was no doubt that the Matterhorn would be our greatest challenge to date.

Since our successful ascent of Mont Blanc the year before, we had discussed several climbing projects, but they had all just been loose ideas. Subconsciously though, I believe we both had decided long ago that this summer would be dedicated to the Matterhorn.

We had read the article, 'When the Unthinkable Happens,' by Soren Pedersen. Who, together with Allan Christensen, tried to climb the Matterhorn in the late 1990s. The article was printed in the Danish outdoor magazine Adventure World and describes a dramatic climb brought to a sudden end when the two Danes witness an Italian guide fall to his death right in front of their eyes. Having experienced this, Soren and Allan decided to turn back, and they have never returned to finish where they left off that day.

Even though I have had numerous chats with Allan when we have met on our annual ice climbing trips to Norway, I have never heard him talk about the Matterhorn. I therefore decided to give him a call one day to learn about the general conditions on the mountain. Some days later, I also contacted Soren to get his opinion. Naturally, none of them were able to talk about the last section of the climb which they had left unexplored, but they both confirmed the information from the guidebook: a labyrinth of loose rocks and difficult route finding.

Weeks went by, and as we gathered information about the mountain, my expectations became overwhelming. I felt convinced that we, technically and physically, had what it would take to be capable of climbing the mountain, but I was also well aware that a successful attempt on the Matterhorn would require all the concentration we could possibly muster. A single mistake could be fatal.

Brian and I know each other well. We have been climbing together for four years, and we have spent many months together during our trips to Sweden, Norway, Bulgaria and France. Through the years, we have spent hours, even days, discussing our experiences as well as the risks involved in climbing. We have matched our ambitions, and we share a similar line of thought when it comes to safety. Together, we have acquired the necessary climbing skills on rock, ice and longer alpine routes on snow and mixed terrain. However, compared to our earlier experiences in the Alps, the challenge of the Matterhorn would primarily be sustained rock climbing and difficult route finding: we had more than 1200 meters of steep climbing coming to us in the thin mountain air.

We decided to use a couple of extended weekends to prepare specifically for what we expected to meet on the Matterhorn. One training weekend took us to Utby near central Gothenburg, Sweden. On a parenthetical note, a raven here ate all our food supplies while we had fun on the rocks. Every little bit! Stupid bird! We spent another weekend in Nissedal in southern Norway which we knew to be a good area to practice route finding and arrange belays. Unexpectedly, we also learnt the value of keeping calm when under pressure. It is not always a simple matter to find the easiest way back after a long day's climb! And on the classic route, 'Via Lara', we got a bit more exercise on the descent than was planned for. Like so many before us (as we have later been told), we had gotten confused by the numerous cairns, and therefore we spent four long hours on the return journey. Through pouring rain, getting our trousers torn by the dense scrub and taking many steps in vain, we reached our car – three hours later than the time those familiar with the route would have arrived at. Through the years we have had many similar experiences, but we never blame each other for the decisions made while on the way. Instead, we evaluate the situation afterwards to aim to be better equipped for future challenges.

During our trips, we spent the evenings discussing preparations for summiting the Matterhorn. Actually, it was unnecessary to confirm our unspoken agreements, but still we repeated them to each other: if one wanted to turn back, we both turned back; we were to be open about our physical and mental conditions on the mountain in order to support each other and utilize our resources the best way possible.

While the trips to Sweden and Norway had offered good and interesting climbing, the days outdoors in the company of Brian had most of all fuelled my yearn to get out there, and whetted my appetite for more challenges and experiences.

I picked up Brian at the train station in Kolding in southern Denmark, where he met me with a broad smile full of expectations. We were pleased and excited, and as was usual practice, we hurried into the car and headed off towards our goal without bothering each other with unnecessary questions concerning the packing list.

The Jeep took in kilometer after kilometer while Brian read out loud from different internet printouts of prior attempts on the Matterhorn.

'Can you hand me your Passport,' I said to him as we approached the German border. He became very still!

'I think I forgot it,' he replied and asked if I thought it would be a problem. I didn't, so we went on. Germany was no problem. It was not until the Swiss border that Brian really started to sweat.

Responsibly I promised to divert the attention of the policemen at the checkpoint by asking silly questions about the road toll. It was a good plan: the policemen got so upset with me not having cash ready for the sticker to put in the windscreen of the car that they told us to go to a small office nearby. Luckily, they spent so much energy telling us off that they forgot to ask us about our Passports. The operation was a success, and Brian and I agreed that we could probably talk our way out of the country again should it be necessary.

After nearly 1400 kilometers, we arrived at 9 pm in the small Alpine village of Täsch where we had planned to spend the night until we could take the train to Zermatt the next day.

Zermatt lies at the foot of the Matterhorn, and it has long ago had to deal with the consequences of being a popular destination for mountaineers and tourists. Thus, cars have been banned in this town, and visitors as well as goods are taken the last ten kilometers from Täsch to Zermatt by train.

Unfortunately, we had to wait until the next day to continue our journey and to get our first sight of the Matterhorn.

Arrival in Zermatt

Sunday, June 29th

We race each other to get out onto the platform at the train station. Besides the tent and our monstrous backpacks, we are carrying sleeping bags and mats, smaller backpacks for the summit attempt and large shopping bags filled with freeze dried foods. Heavily loaded, we stumble out into the city square from where we try to position ourselves to get the first live peek of the Matterhorn. Even though I have seen hundreds of photos of the mountain, I am overwhelmed by the sight. It's amazing!

'It's so beautiful,' I think out loud while I dump my backpack on the worn cobblestones.

'Yes, and huge,' answers Brian.

He is right. Thoughts are rushing through my head. I actually struggle to control the different moods that wash upon me. At first, I am consumed with awe, then enthused with happiness, and finally the doubt creeps in: will we really be able to climb such a demanding mountain? Will the weather conditions give us the necessary window to push for the summit?

'I'll pop down to find a local weather forecast,' says Brian, and rushes off leaving all the bags he has been carrying next to mine.

There is a terrible stink in the square, and I wonder what it is until I see the contents of the gutter behind me. The sheer amazement that struck me when I saw the Matterhorn has caused me to drop my pack beside a pile of horse droppings. Not far from me, three stagecoaches await rich tourists who probably need rides to the best hotels in town. I am amused by the unusual town life. Everywhere, small electric cars are in silent motion: some deliver tourists to hotels at the other end of the street, others deliver mail and groceries. A Japanese tourist guide has gathered his group around him and seems to be explaining practicalities and the programme of the day. Everything is said through a radio: the guide speaks in the microphone of his headset, and the tourists in front of him receive his advice through their earphones. It looks fancy!

'Well, are we ready to go?' asks Brian and tells me that the campsite is located 300 meters down the road.

On the way, he points out the tourist information office where he has found the weather forecast for the coming 5 days. I am excited to find out what kind of weather to expect, and I question him as we walk. While there is some uncertainty related to the forecast, tomorrow seems promising enough: only a few clouds and no wind. We are discussing whether or not to start our first acclimatization trip tomorrow instead of waiting.

'This must be Zermatt's campsite then,' I say to Brian as I point to a number of small tents behind a shed.

The shed happens to be the sanitary and kitchen facilities for the site and also the office of Richard, a retired mountain guide who now runs the campsite. On the site, which is about half the size of a football ground, there are already many tents and climbers, even though it is still early in the season. We greet them and start to unpack the tent. Behind us are two Germans. They look relaxed and seem to accept that their lunch has been disturbed by our arrival and the mouth organ playing Japanese group behind them.

'It's so incredibly big,' says Brian as we later lie on our mats on the grass and gaze towards the Matterhorn.

I can only agree with him. It's absolutely amazing. While the burner is hissing away and we await a cup of well-deserved coffee, we discuss the route on the mountain. We are both surprised by the less than expected amount of snow on the ridge. During planning, we had been somewhat worried about deciding on the first two weeks of July for our trip. The chance of good weather in the Alps is normally higher later in the season.

I ask about the details in the weather forecast, and Brian explains that after tomorrow there will be several days with clouds and precipitation. That, of course, is not so good, but we will just have to be satisfied with what promises to be a good day tomorrow.

'Where do you think we should go tomorrow?' asks Brian.

Before I have time to answer, my attention is caught by two climbers who, marked by the sun and by fatigue, drag themselves onto the campsite. I wonder whether they have climbed the Matterhorn, and I look at Brian who seems to be sharing my thoughts. Poor guys! They hardly manage to dump their bags before I am all over them with questions. Luckily they seem to appreciate our interest, and they tell us their story.

Chris and Will are both in their early thirties and from England. They met in Zermatt a couple of weeks ago, and since none of them had a climbing partner, they decided to climb together. They tell us about their climb on the Matterhorn and solemnly agree that they have just experienced the toughest day of their lives – what encouragement that is! We ask about the conditions on the route and try to make sense of their explanations and advice. They suggest that we should try to get some information from Richard, the owner of the campsite, who, supposedly, has climbed the Matterhorn several hundred times through his almost 30 years as a guide. This is definitely something we will do. We congratulate them again and withdraw to our own tent where we dig out the guide books and start to plan the next few days of acclimatization.

From the literature and from our own experiences in the Alps, we know all about how important it is to accustom the body to the thin air one meets in the high mountains. We have many a time come across mountaineers suffering from altitude sickness due to poor acclimatization. Most recently, on Mont Blanc, we witnessed a Spanish girl with acute symptoms of altitude sickness who was being assisted down by a guide.

It seems an obvious choice to make the Breithorn the target for our first day. With its 4164 meters and location next to the Klein Matterhorn lift, it is the most easily approachable 4000'er in the Alps. This is also the reason why it is a highly regarded one-day project for ordinary tourists who, accompanied by a guide, can make it to the summit in a few hours. The main purpose of our attempt tomorrow is first and foremost acclimatization. We do make an effort, however, to find a different route to the summit than the somewhat trivial normal route, in order to make the climb more interesting. We decided on a slightly steeper route to Breithorn Central Summit as our objective for the first day at altitude.

'If we're to make it to the shops before they close, we'd better get a move on,' Brian suggests.

It is definitely not the first time we have forgotten everything about time and place as we sit with our noses buried in books and maps planning future climbs. As we still need to buy a detailed map and purchase rescue insurance, we must get going.

As we approach the bookshop, we discuss the necessity of buying yet another map. We usually manage with the photos and descriptions in the guide books. We do, however, agree that we need good maps of the area in order to be able to find our way should we get caught in the clouds or in a storm.

Poor Brian! In the book shop he has to put up with my climbing-gear-and-books-syndrome. I always get absolutely euphoric when I am let into shops with climbing gear, and this particular one is full of cool books of great climbs, guide books and maps, too. We end up settling for only one map, which covers the area of the Breithorn and the Matterhorn, along with the indispensable two volumes of Selected Climbs. These guide books are organized like the ones we know from the Mont Blanc area. They offer a rich supply of routes of varying levels of difficulty, information about special conditions and approaches and details about the many alpine huts scattered all over the area.

My good friend Mikkel has explained the requirement for mountain rescue insurance for the Zermatt area. He has told us that, as opposed to some other countries in Europe, you will be charged with all expenses related to being rescued in the mountains in Switzerland. We have never been in a climbing accident in which we needed rescuing, but the 25 euros for the policy seem too little to save should the unfortunate happen.

On our way back to the campsite, we notice a giant cloud that covers most of the upper part of the Matterhorn; exactly as I know it from the many photos of the mountain I have seen while surfing the Internet.

On the campsite we meet Richard, who is making his evening rounds. He takes time to explain the current conditions on the mountain. He tells us that the Hörnli Ridge has probably not been better in 20 years. Normally the route would be covered in snow, but as it is now, he reckons we can climb most of it without crampons. Splendid!

We are quite happy with the outcome of our first day in Zermatt. We have both made the necessary purchases and received heaps of useful information. With above average enthusiasm, we thus approach the last task of the day: cooking!

The First Ascent

The first successful ascent of the Matterhorn was nothing short of spectacular. It is a legendary story that reminds us about the thin line between success and tragedy. In principle, every time a high mountain is climbed successfully for the first time, it is an impressive feat and deserves acknowledgement.

He or she who places their foot on top of a previously unclimbed mountain will make it into the book of mountaineering history. The first successful attempt of the Matterhorn, however, was like nothing else. It was a triumph of mountaineering – and a tragedy!

In 1786, Doctor Paccard and the peasant Balmat succeeded in being the first to climb Mont Blanc. It was a massive endeavor of enormous importance, not only for the small society in Chamonix at the foot of Mont Blanc, but for the whole alpine region. The ascent encouraged many others to try to repeat what Paccard and Balmat had managed to do. As the years went by, more and more of the Alp summits were conquered: mountaineering was in its golden age, and one by one the seemingly unending number of peaks were climbed. The Matterhorn, on the other hand, remained unclimbed!

By 1860, English alpinists had acquired the majority of successful first ascents in the Alps. England led the industrialization and was prospering. Railways and passenger boats gave Englishmen the opportunity to travel and explore, and for some to live out their interest in sports and physical activity. Many of them were teachers who utilized their long vacations to go to the continent to walk and climb. In small alpine villages at the foot of the mountains, they hired local peasants who, for a modest amount of money, joined the foreign adventurers. To the peasants, mountaineering was as new as it was to the ambitious Englishmen. Together they forged ahead and developed usable techniques and simple, but much needed, equipment.

In England, the young Edward Whymper was ignorant of the endeavors of his fellow countrymen in the Alps, and he knew nothing about mountaineering. It is said that he was bored with life in general and dreamt of traveling and seeing new places. In 1860, a publisher sent the 20-year-old Whymper to the Alps and asked him to return with drawings suitable for the publisher's books. Whymper left and was strongly taken by the strange landscape he met on his walks in the valleys. The publisher was pleased with his work and sent him back to the Alps the following year. To Whymper, the mountains quickly became a passion, and the sight of the majestic Matterhorn had given him great ambitions.

At this time, just about every mountaineer of the golden age had given up every thought of climbing the Matterhorn. The most skilful said it was impossible, the most daring and adventurous had withdrawn from the challenge, and it was even said that evil spirits lived on the mountain. The Matterhorn was terrifying!

Whymper was undeterred by this. He headed towards the village of Valtournenche on the Italian side of the Matterhorn. At the same time, one of the few other people who still believed the mountain could be climbed, Professor John Tyndall, headed towards the Matterhorn with his guide. They quickly returned, though, as Tyndall's guide lost his nerve. Simultaneously, Whymper did not succeed in finding men in the town of Breuil who were willing to follow him up on the terrible mountain. At last, however, he did manage to persuade an Italian guide to help him. Together they spent a cold night on the Col du Lion at the foot of the Southwest Ridge, and the following day, they managed to climb only a short way up the mountain before the Italian guide decided to quit. Whymper went home to England, still determined to pursue his dream, and even though he had not yet climbed very high on the mountain, he had become convinced that the Matterhorn could in fact be climbed.

In 1862, Whymper was back. Together with his travel companion, MacDonald, he hired two Swiss guides in Zermatt and began another attempt. But they were soon given up as a storm set in, and the Swiss guides lost their nerve.

Subsequently, Whymper arranged an attempt with Jean-Antoine Carrel – the only mountain guide in town who believed that the Matterhorn could be climbed. As a matter of fact, he had already tried a couple of times, and, being quite arrogant, he thought he was the only one capable of leading such a demanding expedition. Whymper was excited. The first night was spent far above the point where Whymper slept on his first attempt, and he really believed that this time they would make it to the top. But luck was not on their side: Carrel's guide, Pession, became ill, and this ended the promising expedition. Carrel simply refused to go on without Pession, and, at the same time, he was way too proud to climb alone with Whymper, whom he considered an amateur.

Some days later, MacDonald went home, and Whymper set out for his first solo attempt. The climbing was challenging, and on one occasion he had to jump to reach the next hold far above his head. Whymper knew it was foolish to climb alone; yet he pushed on and got as high as 4100 meters. No one had ever been this high on the Matterhorn. That same evening, he was reminded how dangerous the Matterhorn was with every step potentially leading to a fall. On the descent, he slipped and tumbled some 60 meters down loose rocks before he managed to break his fall at the edge of a cliff. He only just avoided the deadly drop that would have sent him more than a thousand meters down towards the glacier. Using his last reserves of will power, he managed to bring himself to a small plateau where he immediately passed out. After this experience, he went back to Breuil where he once again met Carrel. They agreed to give it a new go, but yet another storm sent them back. By now, Whymper was so convinced that the ascent could be made that he arranged one more attempt with Carrel. On the morning of departure, however, Carrel was nowhere to be found. People said that he had gone hunting.

Whymper was disappointed but still firmly determined. He was going to climb that mountain, and he arranged his sixth attempt with a local peasant, Luc Meynet whom he knew from earlier trips. Some would call this small expedition a success: they reached further than anyone before them. But to Whymper it was another disappointment: so close and yet they had to give up due to Meynet's lack of skills.

Back in Breuil, Whymper met Carrel, who had not gone hunting but instead joined a strong group with Professor Tyndall, the guide Bennen and another guide. Whymper had to go back to England but felt that he could not leave until he knew whether this group, the strongest on the mountain so far, would make it to the top. He passed the time in the valley anxiously waiting to hear about the result of this promising attempt. At one point, some thought they saw a flag on the top. Whymper waited. In the evening, the group returned, but as Whymper noted, there was nothing victorious in their appearance. They did not make it, but they had been higher than Whymper. They had turned back only 250 meters below the summit, probably due to a power struggle between Bennen and Carrel. Whymper could now go back to England, and no further attempts to climb the Matterhorn were made in 1862.

In the summer of 1863, Whymper went back to Breuil to arrange a new expedition with Carrel, but the weather prevented them from even setting off.

The relationship between Whymper and Carrel was strange. They respected each other, but first and foremost they were rivals. Most other people were still convinced that climbing the Matterhorn was impossible, and, consequently, Whymper and Carrel needed not worry too much about competition to the top. They therefore ventured on other smaller climbing adventures around the Matterhorn. The strange companions came to know each other well. Whymper wondered why Carrel had never tried to climb the Matterhorn alone; he actually suspected Carrel of nourishing the idea of the impossibility of climbing the Matterhorn in order to make his ultimate success all the better.

In 1864, no attempts were made on the Matterhorn. Instead, Whymper climbed other mountains with the French guide Michel Croz, whom he trusted to have the skills necessary to make a serious attempt on the Matterhorn.

In the season of 1865, Whymper climbed some smaller tops in the Zermatt area while he and Croz awaited the right weather for the final push on the Matterhorn. So far, all attempts had been on the Southwest Ridge, but Whymper had made a discovery on one of his trips in the area: he now believed that the mountain could be climbed from the northeast along the Hörnli Ridge. He believed it to be an illusion that this part of the mountain was too steep to be climbed. Earlier, any idea about attempting an ascent from the Zermatt side of the mountain had been out of the question, and, indeed, Whymper found himself unable to persuade Croz, who thought the Northeast Ridge would be way too dangerous and difficult.

Since it was only early season and the Matterhorn was still covered in ice and snow, they went to Chamonix where Croz had an appointment. Whymper spent time climbing some impressive mountain routes; like a first successful ascent on the Aiguille Verte, a serious 4000 meter peak.

Back in Valtournenche, Whymper told Carrel about his new idea, and Carrel acknowledged it and agreed to join forces with him. Whymper, however, was fooled: Carrel had other plans, and on July 11th, he approached the mountain from the south together with a group of wealthy Italians who had hired him as their guide. Whymper was furious and regretted letting Carrel in on his plans.

At that time, a talented English mountaineer, Lord Francis Douglas, and his young guide Joseph Taugwalder arrived. They both joined Whymper and were supportive of an attempt on the Northeast Ridge. The three departed immediately to Zermatt where they, after meeting up with Josephs' father, Peter Taugwalder senior, and his brother, Peter Taugwalder junior, met Croz. This was in fact a surprise to Whymper. Croz' client had become ill, and Croz had instead been hired by the Reverend Charles Hudson, another talented English mountaineer. Together with another young Englishman, Robert Hadow, they had come to Zermatt to climb the Matterhorn. The two parties agreed to join forces and approach the mountain via the Northeast Ridge.

It was a race to the top. On the Southwest Ridge, Carrel's group moved forward with their expensive, but heavy, equipment displaying a slow, but safe, pace. On the Northeast Ridge, Whymper along with Douglas, Taugwalder Senior, his sons Joseph and Peter Taugwalder, Croz, Hudson and the inexperienced

Hadow, would give it a go. On July 13th at 5.30 am they left Zermatt.

While some of them set up tents at 3300 meters, others in the group went on to make a reconnaissance higher up on the mountain. When they returned and euphorically could tell that they had met no serious obstacles, Whymper felt sure they would make it. On the other hand, he was worried about the group on the other side of the mountain, of whose progress he knew nothing. To Whymper – and probably also to Carrel – these were nerve wracking hours.

The following morning, they forced their way towards the summit. Only Joseph Taugwalder had to turn back. The weather was perfect, and the ridge was exactly as Whymper expected: there was nothing to prevent them from succeeding. After years of unsuccessful attempts, Whymper would proudly be able to plant a flag on the summit of the Matterhorn. But would he be the first one? There were no footprints in the snow. From the top, looking down the south side of the mountain, they saw Carrel and his group only 200 meters below. When they called to them, the Italians immediately turned back. Whymper felt sorry for Carrel. He had wanted them to make it to the summit together, and he knew this was a major disappointment for Carrel.

Whymper spent approximately one hour on the summit together with father and son Peter Taugwalder, Croz, Douglas, Hudson and Hadow before beginning the descent. Before leaving, they placed a bottle containing a note with their names on the summit.

Croz led off followed by Hadow, Hudson, Douglas and Taugwalder Senior and with Whymper and young Taugwalder at the back. After a while, it became more difficult, and they only moved one at a time. Croz guided Hadow, who moved very insecurely. Suddenly he slipped, fell over Croz and they tumbled. Hudson and Douglas were also pulled down before the rope between Douglas and Taugwalder Senior snapped. The four of them slided down the mountain side and disappeared one by one over the north face. On the ridge remained Whymper, Taugwalder Senior and young Taugwalder, all deeply shocked. It was quite some time before Whymper got them moving again. On stiff legs they stumbled along and Whymper feared that they would fall too.

Finally, they found a spot on the mountain where they could spend this cold and sad night. Early the next morning, they descended to Zermatt to convey the sad message. The town was shocked and went into a state of grief.

The following day, the bodies of Croz, Hadow and Hudson were found, and some days later, they were moved to Zermatt by the aid of 21 mountain guides. On that same day, Carrel finally climbed the Matterhorn from the Italian side via the Southwest Ridge.

The body of Douglas has never been found.

The news spread quickly around the globe. The story made front page headlines everywhere, and in England it was in newspaper leaders for several days. No other event in the world of mountaineering has ever matched this interest. After the terrible accident, which cost the lives of three Englishmen and a Frenchman, many advocated the banning of mountaineering. Eventually, Queen Victoria of England had to do something, and she asked Lord Chamberlain if mountaineering could be prohibited. Fortunately, it never came that far.

Later on, an investigation was initiated to find out if any of the survivors could be held liable for the accident, but charges could not be raised.

Whymper and Carrel reconciled and became close friends. Together, they went on a successful expedition to the Andes.

The Visitor's Book

I

In the Visitor's Book in The North Wall Bar in Zermatt, you can read authentic accounts of numerous ascents of the Matterhorn. These short stories are authored by the climbers themselves, and when you read them, you come to understand that, for many, this was a lifelong goal. For some, this goal ended in tragedy.

An Amazing Mountain

Having looked at the first part of the route last week, we felt confident that our 5:30 am start from the hut would get us up past the "bimblies" early on and still give us lights and a path in the snow to follow.

All went well, passing through the snowline at 3500 meters. After about two hours we were approaching the Solvay Hut. Then we caught the Spanish contingent, who was desperate not to let us pass.
At the lower Moseley Slab, a group of Poles wearing demolition helmets had their crampons on and were ineffectively scratching snow covered rocks. Time for

the Brits to adopt climbing-through, over and on tactics; which we did, quite unashamedly.

A thick covering of soft, powdery snow above the Solvay made life really hard. The final slopes became "interesting", with little or nothing to grip in the soft covering. Summit time: 6 hours.

The soft snow took ages in descent; 6 hours to the Solvay and we just about reached the easy ground as darkness hit. We arrived back at the Hörnli Hut at 9:45 pm. There are still many on the hill including the demolition crew.

We really feel we've earned this summit. Okay, it took us a long time, and we're still knackered the next evening, but we did it and overcame a shed load of obstacles - and had one brilliant, clear day out of eight. A brilliant mountain, hard earned! Without a guide to make all the decisions and find the route, makes it a truly special, personal experience.

Martin Sluce, Cumbria, UK
Steve Birchall, Stockport, UK
August 20th, 2003

Acclimatizing on Breithorn Central Summit

Monday, June 30th

The town is quiet and cold. With our hats pulled down to cover our ears, we head towards the lift station. We have yet to get a full overview of the timetables for the different lifts but feel safe assuming that there is a departure around 8 am.

As we walk, we talk about what to expect from this first day in the mountains. The Klein Matterhorn lift will, through two middle stations, take us up to 3820 meters from where we will walk for a couple of hours to the foot of Breithorn Central Summit. We are looking forward to getting started but are also well aware that we will feel weak and slow in the thin air waiting for us higher up. On our alpine trips during the last three years, we have acclimatized in the Mont Blanc area. Usually we spend the first couple of days at around 3500 meters. We therefore anticipate that the additional altitude planned for today and the lower level of oxygen will impact both our lungs and muscles, and it is likely to cause a headache. However, we also know that the days following this one will be much easier as the body reacts by beginning to produce more red blood cells to aid the transport of oxygen around the body.

At the bakery, we hastily pick up breakfast, as we run through town to the lift station. But we have run in vain as the lift is not yet open. We sit down on our backpacks in front of the empty station, and while we eat, we are amused by the fact that the Swiss wash and scrub the pavements rather than just using a broom to sweep like we would do in Denmark. The result, however, is perfect!

We meet two Englishmen who tell us that they are heading for the Matterhorn. They want to take advantage of the perfect weather conditions to aid a speedy ascent on the mountain. They plan to climb to the Solvay Hut high up on the ridge and spend the night there. Tomorrow they will finish the climb and try to make it back to Zermatt before nightfall. I respect their enthusiasm, but I do not like their plan of using the Solway Hut. It is an emergency hut, and so it has room for a few people only. As the forecast for tomorrow is also a bit dodgy, I think their plan is somewhat stupid. I ask them if they have read the latest weather forecast. They have not. They regard the Zermatt forecasts as unreliable and have therefore decided not to check them. We tell them what we know from the forecast and wish them a good climb.

As the lift rises up the mountainside, we have a good view of the Matterhorn. With our noses pressed flat against the gondola windows, we take in the scenery. It is amazing! And huge! From here, the mountain seems enormous, and I find it easy to understand why people were convinced for many years that the Matterhorn could not be climbed. At the same time, I can almost sense the emotions that drove Whymper, Tyndall, Carrel and Croz to keep trying.

'My first aid kit is in the top pocket of my pack,' I explain to Brian.

'OK, so is mine,' he replies.

We always let each other in on the contents of our packs to help us find bandages and medicine in case of emergency. In this way, we aim to prepare ourselves for the potential situation that one of the packs is lost or one of us is so badly hurt that he cannot talk to the other. In addition to our normal first aid equipment, my kit also includes an emergency blanket and my mobile phone with the number of the rescue service stored in its memory.

The cold bites at our faces as we step out of the lift at the Klein Matterhorn top station. The long corridor through the mountain is like a giant wind tunnel, and the chill forces us to put on our jackets immediately. For a short moment, I dream of my warm sleeping bag down in Zermatt and suggest this alternative to Brian. He just laughs and begins babbling about the difference between acclimatization at 1620 meters and what we will achieve by climbing the central summit at over 4000 meters. The professor has spoken once again!

I carefully tighten my gaiters, make sure my crampons are buckled correctly and proceed to uncoil the rope. We could probably start off without being tied into the rope, but after only a few hundred meters we will step out onto the broken part of the glacier. Here the rope will be an essential part of our safety.

‘Are we ready?’ asks Brian.

‘Yep!’

After ten minutes of walking, we reach the entrance to the Breithorn Plateau and head towards our route on the Central Summit. Even though the route is neither long nor demanding, we would like to get started as soon as possible in order to make it to the top and return before the snow on the south face has been softened too much by the sun.

Whereas the track towards Breithorn is wide and clear, there are no footprints towards the Central Summit. We pause for a short while to discuss the right direction. From the Klein Matterhorn lift it seemed obvious to walk directly towards the route, but from here it is clear to us that this is not going to work. Our first challenge will be to find a safe way through the labyrinth of crevasses which prevent us from walking in a straight line.

From now on, we must keep the rope tight between us at all times to prevent any minor falls from becoming serious. I carefully step onto the untouched snow while Brian follows 12 meters behind me. On several occasions I have to stop to test the snow in front of me with my axe. Will it carry my weight? We are still close enough to the normal route to be able to see the guides pulling the tourists along on their ropes. I fully respect the many people that choose to spend a day of their summer vacations experiencing the mountains. At the same time, I am pleased that our adventure is slightly more isolated.

We approach the beginning of the route, and both of us notice the bergschrund between this part of the glacier and the steeper mountainside. This crevasse, produced by the movement of the glacier, seems fairly easy to pass. In the middle it is wide open, thus allowing us to gaze down into the seemingly never-ending nothing. Towards the sides, the crevasse is covered by a treacherous layer of snow on which a careless crossing can be very dangerous. Brian prepares to belay me while I search for a suitable place to pass the bergschrund.

'On belay,' says Brian.

I concentrate on keeping my balance while trying to get the axe to bite in the ice on the other side of the crevasse.

'OK, are you ready?' I ask Brian

'I've got you!'

After a hard pull on my axe and a controlled kick, I safely cross the gap.

'I'll place an anchor here, and then you can take over the lead!' I shout to Brian.

I take another couple of steps and find a good spot for a belay. I can now securely hold Brian as he crosses the crevasse and continues leading up the route.

'I need all your ice screws,' requests Brian.

He has passed the bergschrund effortlessly and is now ready to lead the first pitch. The route is not so hard and so allows us the possibility of climbing it by moving together. This technique is much faster, but it also requires much more equipment than we have brought. We decide to climb the first pitch in the traditional style which implies that the leader places the equipment and is belayed by the second climber. When the leader has used up the available rope, he will prepare a new belay point from where he will bring up the second. The second removes the equipment as he moves towards the leader.

While Brian is climbing, I notice a group of clouds moving in on the Breithorn massif. It is not really a problem. The route is straight forward, and we will always be able to find our way back to the lift station by using the compass should the clouds close in and prevent us from backtracking easily. On the other hand, we would rather not have a storm develop above us on this exposed terrain.

Brian is now so far above me that we only communicate by shouting, even though it is almost quiet. I hear nothing but the noise from his axe placements and the sound of chunks of ice that fall away as he climbs. This is one of the moments I venture into the mountains to experience: you allow your mind to wander while you enjoy the amazing scenery. I try to name the different summits but could do with some assistance of a map or guide book.

'On belay!' shouts Brian.

I now know that he is safely tied to an anchor and that I can begin to dismantle the anchor at my end.

'You may climb!' he shouts.

These shouting routines are an important part of the safety chain when climbing, for us and as well as for all other climbers: by using the same commands every time, misunderstandings are avoided. The different commands signal which procedure has just been completed as well as inform how to proceed. I answer Brian and I start climbing. I immediately feel that he tightens the rope between us.

Although the route is not particularly steep, it is steep enough to force us to use the front point of our crampons. This technique is used when it is not possible to place the entire foot on the slope. Instead, the front of the boot is kicked hard into the ice to make the spikes on the front of the crampon bite into the frozen surface.

I enjoy our climb, and for a moment I forget the trouble of breathing in the thin air. For some reason, I tend to forget the lack of oxygen on the more technically demanding sections of a route, whereas I often feel burdened by the lack of oxygen on the easier walking passages when acclimatizing.

When I reach Brian, I mention that I think we will soon be rather isolated within a giant cloud that is getting close, and I suggest that we use a couple of minutes to memorize the terrain to prepare us for a safe descent in reduced visibility. Brian has also seen the cloud, and he suggests that we skip the planned break and hurry to the summit from where we can traverse to the easily identifiable track on the normal route to Breithorn.

After an hour, we reach the summit. I belay Brian on the last pitch while, at the same time, I stamp out a platform on which we can both stand comfortably. The visibility has decreased dramatically during the last 15 minutes. We can only see five or, sometimes, ten meters in front of us, and the few instances that allow a glimpse of sunlight to pass through the clouds are very brief. I have used these windows, however short they were, to memorize the ridge in order for us to walk a safe distance from the edge to avoid the fragile cornices. It has been impossible, though, to get an overview of all the crevasses, and we will have to be careful.

I forcefully place my axe in the snow, move one foot and then the other. It is a steep passage. I try to maintain a steady pace to avoid pulling Brian out of balance by sudden movements as he keeps the eight meters of rope tight between us.

'Look out! There's a big crevasse on our right,' I warn.

'OK!'

I feel confident that we are walking in the right direction. At the same time, I really do not know when to make a left turn to reach the Breithorn Plateau. However, given the aggressive slope of the terrain, it is safer to traverse too far than to turn too soon as it would send us out onto the very steep sections to the left of the route we have climbed.

Suddenly I hear voices. They have to come from people on the normal route to Breithorn. Perhaps we are close?

'Look!' I yell to Brian and point towards the plateau below us.

Someone has had the mercy to give us a window lasting just long enough for us to see all the way to the Klein Matterhorn lift, and to realize that we are only about 75 meters from the safe track on the normal route.

As we walk towards the lift station, we curse our weak physique. The pulse is high, and it is hard to accept that it takes so much effort just to walk. We know that tomorrow will be better, but it is frustrating – like being trapped in the body of a 90-year old!

'Is your head aching?' asks Brian in the lift back down to Zermatt.

'A little, but I'm sure that a couple of liters of water will make me feel much better,' I answer.

'Yeah, and a coke!'

No doubt, but first we need to see the weather forecast for the coming few days, hanging in the window of the tourist information office. It is easy enough to understand the computer drawn images of mountains and dark clouds with water drops. It is quite a different story with the written German forecast. We approach the information desk inside to get some help. The helpful lady behind the desk struggles to find the correct technical terms in English, but with a mix of Danish, German and English, we get a picture that matches the illustration in the window. This settles the discussion: the first day of rest this season will be tomorrow – regrettably.

Altitude Sickness

Altitude sickness is a dangerous condition which, in its acute state, may cause death for those who ignore the symptoms. Planning to climb a mountain requires knowledge about the different types and phases of altitude sickness. Acclimatization is a must to prepare the body for the inevitable lack of oxygen at altitude.

When a mountaineer does any kind of activity in the mountains, he or she will experience trouble getting enough oxygen into their system. This is a consequence of the amount of oxygen in the air dropping as height is gained. Fortunately, the body is able to compensate for the shortage of oxygen, but it takes time. It is advised that, when moving above 3000 meters, one should not increase the sleeping height by more than 500 meters per night. Even with these precautions, some people will feel symptoms of altitude sickness, such as headache, fatigue, lack of appetite, nausea and vomiting.

For a mountaineer it is therefore important to be able to recognize the signals from the body, since even minor symptoms may worsen quickly if one continues ascending. In a worst case scenario, symptoms may develop into deadly oedemas: brain oedema which implies that fluid collects around the brain or lung oedema which is effusion of fluids into the lungs, which may cause the mountaineer to drown from within.

The chance of a successful ascent is therefore closely connected to a well planned and executed acclimatization. On high mountains like the Matterhorn, a lot of people will experience symptoms of altitude sickness, and some will risk their lives without the necessary acclimatization. It is standard procedure for experienced mountaineers to spend up to a week on other, lower mountains, allowing the body to adjust to the lower oxygen levels, before they set out for the actual target mountain. Scientific medical knowledge about altitude sickness is still relatively new, and even though a lot has been written about the topic, it is far from described completely. Across the world, research is being done to map causes, prevention and treatment of altitude sickness. Everyone agrees, however, that altitude sickness is best prevented through acclimatization.

The Visitor's Book
II

Just My Opinion

Headed up to the Matterhorn yesterday, bivouacked, and then started climbing the Hörnli Ridge at 5 am this morning. People come to Zermatt to do the Matterhorn via the Hörnli Ridge because 'it is a classic'. I'm sitting here now after doing the route - and no 'it is not a classic'. A classic does not start with loose rock all over the place and end with a line of guides and clients - you included - waiting for your turn on the fixed ropes leading to the top.

When you get to the top then the problems really begin. Descending the Matterhorn is probably the worst descent that I have ever experienced. Today I witnessed a fellow climber fall to his death down the east face. Maybe you can say that this has altered my opinion of the Matterhorn. Reading this will probably not change your mind on whether or not you want to climb the Matterhorn, so if you are going to climb it, please be careful and don't become one more of the deaths connected with the Matterhorn.

Frank Cox, Ireland
August 20th, 2002

A Hut in the Mountains

Wednesday, July 2nd

'There is no way this is going to dry before we leave. We'll have to take it down while it's still wet,' exclaims Brian as we try to shake the rain off the tent.

After a rather dull and rainy day of rest yesterday, we are now preparing for a longer stay in the mountains. We are far from convinced that the weather will be better higher up, but as the weather forecast can be interpreted this way, we have decided that this is it!

Yesterday was spent on thorough research. We have identified three interesting summits which differ in degrees of difficulty and which can all be reached from the small, primitive Rossi Volante Hut located at 3750 meters on the Italian side of the Breithorn Massif. In the hut we should find mattresses and blankets, but we may also find a hut filled with snow if the door or windows have been left open or have been damaged in a storm. We add our sleeping bags and mats to our packs already heavily laden with climbing gear, extra clothing and gloves, water bottles, a stove and freeze dried foods for four days. We have not decided exactly how long to be gone, but three days seem probable. The extra food rations are meant as a backup in case the weather prevents us from returning on day three.

It is 6.50 am and we are still packing. While Brian struggles with the wet tent, I try to divide the rest of our gear into two piles. One to take on the mountain and one to leave in a storage room at the train station together with the tent.

From the lift, we get another look at the east wall of the Matterhorn. Our plan is to use the Northeast Ridge, the so-called Hörnli Ridge. Every time we get the chance, we try to get an impression of what awaits us. The view today is very different from what we saw two days ago. The day before yesterday, we were satisfied with the limited amount of snow, but a lot has happened since then. Even though it is impossible to see exactly how much snow has actually fallen, there is no doubt that the bare wall from yesterday is now covered in white. This is pretty bad news, although we do not plan to climb the mountain for another week. Our first priority is to prepare for the summit ascent and to be as well acclimatized as possible.

I remember the two Englishmen we met, who planned to climb the Matterhorn during Monday and Tuesday, and I ask Brian what he thinks about their current situation. Since Monday noon the mountain has been hidden in clouds – the result of which we have just witnessed. We both doubt they have made it to the top. It is terribly frustrating to have been told about somebody's coming adventure when you will probably never learn how it went.

'Do you think we should have stuck to the bottom of the plateau?' I ask Brian.

We have chosen to follow a line higher up the mountainside. According to the map, this will bring us to the Rossi Volante Hut from above, and in that way we will avoid having to climb several hundred meters back up from the plateau lower down. On the map it seems straightforward, but we are now facing a labyrinth of crevasses and are discussing the sensibility of our plan. Below us we spot three men who, apparently, are also heading for the hut. The packs they are carrying seem to be too heavy for just a day-trip. Brian recognizes them as the three Irishmen who arrived at the campsite yesterday.

We agree that the many crevasses are an unnecessary risk which can easily be avoided by backtracking a little way and then seeking down to the tracks on the plateau. It is annoying to lose altitude, but we are determined to take the detour. We also agree that yesterday's interpretation of the map was probably a bit too creative! We hurry down to the tracks and begin gaining on the Irishmen. We progress faster than they do; it is great to feel the difference between today and our first day in the mountains.

'Are you sure the Irishmen only arrived yesterday?' I ask Brian.

'Positive. I suppose it's somewhat risky to spend the first night at this altitude', he answers.

'My thoughts exactly!' To sleep at 3750 meters is pretty damn high for a first day at altitude. I have often thought about doing it but have never dared to. The risk of altitude sickness is increased, and even though it would mean fewer trips with the lifts, I believe the risk is not worth taking. Even though the consequences may not be severe, the milder symptoms of altitude sickness like diarrhea and migraine-like headaches are sufficient to spoil any preparations.

Another hour and we will be at the hut. I look forward to lunch and the primitive life in the hut with cozy nights, the constant roar of the gas stove, the hours passed by reading the visitors' book and the endless discussions about future – near and distant – climbing trips. It will be great!

'Look out! There's a hidden crevasse here,' I warn Brian.

'Right! Do you need me to belay you?' he asks.

'Yeah, but I'll need a couple of meters of slack rope.'

'OK, just a second,' he replies.

While Brian is searching for a spot to place his axe, I look for a suitable point that will let me pass without having to make too demanding acrobatic maneuvers.

'You're on belay,' says Brian.

I stand at the edge of the crevasse and try to chop away the thin snow bridge that hides the crevasse in order to estimate how far I will have to jump to make it to the other side. I tell Brian that I am going for it, and I take a couple of steps backwards before launching myself forward with my axe above my head. As I land, I slam the axe hard into the snow to prevent me from falling backwards. Right by the book, I think, and send Brian a satisfied smile. I see that he is struggling to release his axe. That is a good sign. That axe and its hold in the snow was my primary protection only a few seconds ago.

Brian now follows. For him, the second climber, the procedure is a little different. He approaches the crevasse and the spot from which I jumped. I continue down the track to make sure that there are no other crevasses to fall into on this side. On Brian's signal, we will both start running while making sure that the rope between us is kept tight.

'Can I have a couple of meters of slack?' Brian asks.

I go back towards the crevasse to give him enough rope to enable him to pick up some pace, and prepare to run. The idea is that I must run just as explosively as Brian. This will allow me to drag him over the crevasse should he stumble, or if his jump is too short. I must be ready to place my axe in the snow and throw my bodyweight over it if he should fall into the crevasse.

'Perfect, just by the book!' I exclaim.

The weather is almost ideal, a mix of blue sky and scattered cumulus give a pleasant cool temperature. The terrain slopes upwards, and we are reminded once again that we are moving at altitude. Above us, we can both see and hear the Irish climbers. They take turns at swearing, and it seems that their undertaking is not exactly a walk in the park. I can now see what they are doing: the last bit up to the rocks is steep. One of them seems quite confident and moves freely on his crampons. The other two, however, certainly seem to feel the exposure of the situation, and they focus all of their resources on the next step.

'Shit! I lost the bloody water!'

A water bottle shoots down the slope towards us. It flies right by me and continues towards Brian. A few meters behind him it slows down before coming to a stop at the edge of a crevasse.

'Let's get it,' Brian suggests, and he starts down-climbing to the left of the track.

I follow him while I keep the rope tight between us. The bottle has come to rest ten meters below us, and since there is no apparent risk involved in fetching the bottle, I agree that we should help the Irishmen. Brian fastens the bottle to his belt with a quickdraw, and we resume the ascent. The Irish climbers are still on the middle of the glacier and demonstrate an impressive vocabulary of foul language. We say 'hi' to them and continue up and past them. I do not find this section difficult. Not at all, actually, but I do understand that climbers with little or no experience would find it intimidating. It does not look as if the two struggling Irishmen have tried this technique before. I pass around the first rocks and put Brian on belay. We ask them if they are all right, and since they confirm this, we continue.

The next pitch involves scrambling over rock using our axes and crampons. The pick of the axe is placed in the thin cracks of the rock, and the crampons are rested on small contours of the sloping surface. Although the technique is a bit unusual, it is rather efficient, and the sharp axe and pointy crampons provide much better grip on wet or icy rock than the soles of big mountain boots.

'This is quite a mouthful for our new friends below,' says Brian.

We decide to wait and see how they get on. The guy who led on the ice is also leading on the rock, and does it well. It does not take him long to reach us, and from here he belays his mates. No panic. We proceed to check out the hut. The last 20 meters are straightforward. The many previous visitors have left clear marks.

There are crampon scratches all over the place leading us to the entrance of the hut. Part of the hut is built on an aluminum frame and stands very exposed right on the edge of the cliff. A gaze down reveals a drop of more than one hundred meters.

'It's a small castle,' I state enthusiastically, as I open the outer shutters.

The hut is approximately three by four meters and sleeps eight or ten people on two wide wooden platforms. On one side there is a huge bulge under two mattresses. Closer investigation reveals that the hut has sunk, and the floor has been broken and pushed up into the sleeping accommodation. On the top shelf is a pile of blankets. Wonderful! By a window are a table and two benches, and the wooden floor bears the signs of the passing of many cramponed feet. In the middle of the floor is a fire mark, suggesting an incidence of cooking getting slightly out of hand.

'This is so cool,' comments Brian.

I agree. We dump the climbing gear and immediately begin to organize the contents of our packs. If the weather holds, we plan to climb Roccia Nera this afternoon. This small peak rises to 4075 meters directly above the hut.

Despite the fact that we have only known Peter, Phil and Mark for less than one hour, we are already enjoying each others' company. Peter, who is the most experienced, tells us about their plan of staying one night and of hopefully climbing Castor at 4228 meters tomorrow. This afternoon, they might give Roccia Nera a go, like us, although making it to the hut has been a tough experience for Phil and Mark. After some discussion, they agree to postpone the decision until this afternoon and spend the next couple of hours just hanging out in the hut.

'Tell me, is this snow or ice from the glacier, you have brought me?' questions Brian. He is melting snow over the stove for water for our drinking bottles.

'There may be all sorts of surprises in there, Brian!' I reply.

I have collected the snow from the plateau above the hut. It was impossible to find any fresh snow, so instead I used my helmet to scrape the thin layer of older snow on top of the ice into a plastic bag. And now that Brian has melted the first portion, it is evident that the snow contained some finely grained rubble, which has now settled at the bottom of the pot. We decide that there is no big health risk involved if we boil it well and filter it before we drink it.

Neither of us expect much from climbing Roccia Nera, but we agree that any activity at this altitude is a good thing. After a few hours in the hut, we are ready to move off. Peter and Phil have also decided to give it a go, whereas Mark chooses to stay in the hut. Apparently, he has injured his leg on the way to the hut, and he also complains of a headache and of not feeling at his best. Trying to climb Roccia Nera will most likely only make him feel worse.

I find it fascinating that, after only one day in the thin air, we perform so much better than we did on Monday. Despite the rather steep ascent on Roccia Nera, I feel really good and thoroughly enjoy the climb. A glance at my altimeter tells me that we have already climbed 100 meters. So far, we have not placed any protection. We are tied into the rope and move together.

I can still see Phil and Peter below us. They started a bit later and seem to have chosen a route further right on the face. The weather is now overcast, and the summit is hidden in a thick blanket of clouds.

According to my altimeter, we are only 50 meters below the summit, but I cannot see anything. The distance between Brian and me is only 12 meters, and yet I lose sight of him from time to time. We evaluate whether or not we should continue and agree that the weather as such is not a problem as long as we take care not to get too close to the edge. We have both seen photos of the mountain and know that the biggest risk is getting too close to the precipitous drop down the southeast wall.

'I think we need to go further to the right,' I suggest to Brian as I try to recall the photo from the guide book.

'Yeah, and definitely before we reach the ridge which, according to the book, is often corniced,' answers Brian and asks whether I can see the ridge?

'No, but I'm sure we are close. I think we should start traversing to the right!'

What a surprise it is that this ascent has ended up like a small expedition, I think to myself while moving on towards what I believe is the summit. I can no longer see Brian - only hear him. There is no wind at all. It is like being in a vacuum.

'Can you see the summit?' asks Brian after a couple of minutes.

'I think so, but if it's a cornice, we have to be really careful,' I reply and take the last couple of steps towards the top of Roccia Nera.

We laugh about the situation: on the two summits we have been on so far, we have had no view whatsoever. In my opinion, the view from the top of a mountain is part of the reward for the effort. I hope that we will at least be granted a 360 degree panorama on the Matterhorn.

The descent is surprisingly difficult and requires a great deal more concentration than I had imagined. The limited amount of snow on the mountain and the freezing conditions have made the surface very hard, and we struggle to find our ascending tracks. We decide to move one at a time while focusing on not getting too close to the steep southeast wall. We invent a technique which implies using almost the entire width of the mountain: Brian uses his axe as protection while he belays me as I climb down. When there is no more rope, we change roles, and I place my axe as protection and belay Brian. He moves in an arch around and below me. It is fast but also somewhat risky as it would result in a rather dangerous pendulum movement in case of a fall. On the other hand, we are sure that neither of us will fall far.

'There they are!' Peter shouts to Phil as they point towards us.

Finally, we are below the clouds, and the visibility allows us to see all the way to the rocks above the hut where the two Irishmen wait for us. They had become worried and decided to go look for us. We acknowledge their concern and explain about the difficulties we had in terms of finding the summit. Under normal conditions, the summit should be reached in an hour from the hut, and the descent shouldn't take much more than half that. We used three hours in total, but it was worth it, as it has added to our growing mountain experience and will help us make appropriate decisions in future situations.

Back in the hut, Peter informs us that none of them felt well, which is why they had decided to turn back half way up. Mark's condition has not improved, and they talk about canceling their plan of climbing Castor and instead return to Zermatt the following morning.

Brian is reading the guide book and talks with enthusiasm about the Southwest Ridge of Pollux, a nearby peak at 4092 meters. He suggests we climb it tomorrow. It is not completely dark outside yet, and we go out onto the balcony of the hut to study the mountain and compare it with the description in the guide book. From our position, there is only a kilometer or so to where the route begins.

'The guidebook suggests an alternative, more direct, route which leads up over an ice wall,' says Brian, and he asks me if I can see the ice wall.

I can. I try hard to imagine how the route continues above that ice wall. The route starts with steep ice leading to a series of rock pitches, much like what we will experience on the Matterhorn. The final pitches are on an exposed snow ridge. Amazing!

'I'm in! When do we start?' I ask.

'The book says an hour and a half for the climb, and I think it will take us almost an hour to get there,' answers Brian. With reference to the Roccia Nera climb, he suggests we add an extra hour.

‘So that’s three to four hours for the ascent and maybe two to three hours to return to the hut. Let’s say we leave the hut at about 7 am and make it a morning climb,’ I suggest.

We plan to get up at 5.30 and ask the Irishmen if they are okay with that. They are. They also plan for an early start hoping for an attempt on Castor. However, they are not too optimistic regarding Mark’s condition, and the two others also admit to feeling the altitude. Despite this, we all keep our spirits high, and all contribute with stories from past adventures – some of which are less true than others. We are taken by the atmosphere and do our best to try to match their stories. Phil asks about our Matterhorn plans. He is convinced that we will make it and promises to follow our endeavor through his binoculars from the campsite. Great guys! It is as if we have known them forever. The fact that we have a common interest and attitude towards being in the mountains, as well as a similar humor, helps greatly. The situation helps too, of course: five men cramped in a hut balanced on the edge of a cliff at 3750 meters.

Despite the heat generated by the stove, the hut is cold. I set the alarm to wake us at 5.30 am and disappear into my sleeping bag.

Mountain Guide Herbert Lüthi

In many alpine villages, not least those around the Matterhorn, the mountain guides, who, week after week, set out to climb the high mountains such as the Matterhorn, are highly regarded. The guides are well aware of the responsibility involved in their job and know that they are part of the very identity of the small village societies.

When mountain guide Herbert Lüthi (born 1960) talks about his values, about life and about his experiences, it is all centered around the mountains.

He was originally trained as a mechanic, and when he first came to Zermatt in 1984, it was to fill a vacant position at a local garage. He had already climbed his first 4000'er and was a passionate skier.

In 1990, he made a decision that changed his life. He wanted to become a guide. He wanted a life which gave him the opportunity to enthuse others with his love for the mountains. To Herbert, it has been a dream come true that he can now make a living by doing what he enjoys best.

In July 2001, Herbert took his first client to the Matterhorn. Herbert had been accepted at the mountain guide school and thus qualified to guide on the mountain. Knowing what happened on this first trip, you will understand that it could easily have been his last. You will also understand that a good guide may be the best life insurance you will ever get.

Herbert Lüthi explains that even a guide who has been on the Matterhorn ten times before, may experience trouble finding the right way. Despite the fact that Herbert had climbed the Matterhorn before, he struggled on this first attempt as a guide. The first part of the climb went well, but Herbert thought they were behind schedule and asked another guide on the route what he thought. The guide told Herbert not to worry; they did not have far to go before the summit.

Near the summit, by the statue of Saint Bernard, his client fell. The Japanese client was saved by Herbert holding the rope. Nevertheless, it did not take long before the exhausted client fell again. Normally, a guide will turn back when a client has a second fall, but with only a short pitch to the summit, Herbert decided to continue. He told the client to muster all his concentration. Carefully, they approached the summit, but with only a few meters to go, the client fell again; he simply tumbled over the edge. Luckily, the Japanese man was a small guy, and Herbert managed to stay on his feet and pull the guy back up. Herbert was shaken up, but also relieved that he had reacted so quickly and thus prevented the Japanese man from pulling him down. Had this happened, they would probably both have fallen to their deaths. But Herbert's work was far from over. Standing on the summit of the Matterhorn at 4478 meters, they still had to descend. Once more, Herbert told his client to focus. Communication was limited as the Japanese man only knew a few polite words in English. From the summit to the Solvay hut, the client fell again, but Herbert managed to break the fall. By the Upper Moseley Slab, however, they ran out of luck. The Japanese man suffered his fifth fall, and this time he broke his leg and had to be evacuated by helicopter. Herbert felt bad that he did not manage to avoid the accident, but was also extremely pleased that the expedition was over. It had been a nightmare.

Since that day, Herbert has guided many clients on the Matterhorn. Even though he is now an experienced guide, he knows that every climb requires all his concentration. Every now and then, he still struggles to find the right way, and almost every time he is on the mountain, he witnesses helicopters rescuing injured climbers.

Herbert Lüthi calls the Matterhorn 'the Graveyard of Mountaineering' as he thinks about the three friends he has lost on the mountain since 1984. Maybe these friends receive a sad thought everytime Herbert, like other guides, places a small crystal at the foot of an iron cross on the Matterhorn.

The Visitor's Book

III

The Longest Day

We left Zermatt to walk up to the Hörnli Hut. The weather was beautiful, and it was going to be that way for 2-3 days. Graham was very keen to get up to the hut, but I was not going to rush, probably because I couldn't.

The next morning we followed the torches at 4:15 am making slow but steady progress. Everybody else seems to be in a hurry, but to us the quality of the scrambling was too good to rush. We reached the Solvay Hut about midday, still quite comfortable in ourselves but moving slowly. Thoughts of turning back were at the back of our minds. No weather problems, however, no problems with the route, so why? We finally reached the summit, and it was only 10 o'clock. But why was it dark? We took the time for a couple of photos, and to marvel at the view of the lights in Zermatt and Breuil. We wondered how many others had seen the view at this time of night.

The climb down was done in the same style as the ascent - very slowly and carefully. At just after 4 am we saw lots of little lights beginning the long climb below us. Hope they managed a good night's sleep! We finally reached the Hörnli Hut at 6 pm the following evening, tired, thirsty and hungry. After one hour's rest, we continued the descent to Zermatt, arriving at 1.00 am.

Was this the longest ascent of the Matterhorn...38 hours?? We hope so.

Andrew Brown, UK
Graham Doodey, UK
August 16th, 2001

Mental Acclimatization at 4092 meters

Thursday, July 3rd

It is 8.15 am and we have only just pulled ourselves out of our sleeping bags. There are only a few spots of sky visible through the dense clouds. It does not seem at all like there is going to be any change in the weather conditions for many hours to come. We track the atmospheric pressure constantly. It has fallen since yesterday, and right now there are only 637 millibars. The pressure will rise when better weather is on its way, but it is going to take a while.

When I went shivering out of the hut to eye the weather conditions at 5.30 am, Brian had mumbled something and asked about the verdict. When I said it looked bad, his only reply was, 'OK, we'll wait'. This was probably a good decision.

As the weather is now, we will still have time to climb the mountain and not have to worry about the snow softening in the sun. Hence, given the current conditions on Pollux, there will be no difference between walking in the morning and in the afternoon.

As always, breakfast is muesli mixed with milk powder, water and sugar. Unless we want it served as porridge, all we need to do is get some snow, melt it, boil it thoroughly, filter it and cool it down... and then breakfast can be served! The first cups of hot water are used for coffee, though. A couple of hours are easily spent on nothing. Yeah well, we're not in a hurry.

Peter informs us that they have decided to return to Zermatt. Both Phil and Mark are suffering because of the altitude. It seems like a good call. Mark does not look good at all after a long night with diarrhea and little sleep. I am sure it will take a couple of days to recover fully. I give Phil my phone number, and he promises to send us a text message in case the weather forecast all of a sudden calls for an attempt on the Matterhorn. I sense that he will double check every forecast and do his very best to keep us informed. It is sad to see them leave; they have been great company. I look forward to seeing them again, and we agree to have a couple of beers when we meet back in Zermatt.

While our company departs, I begin to examine an old fleece that we found in the hard snow during our descent yesterday. The jacket is frozen, and I have to use force to get access to the pockets to see if I can find anything that may identify the owner. After a brief fight, I find a muesli bar in one pocket and a lighter in the other. Brian laughs when I try to date our find. It is no easy task for an amateur archaeologist: muesli bars do not go out of date easily, and the design of the ordinary, disposable lighter has not changed for as long as I can remember. I hang the fleece in the hut, leave the lighter on the table and eat the bar.

The weather is rather stable but still overcast. Hours have passed without any sign of the sun. As there are no signs of wind either, we decide to give Pollux a go. We pack the essentials: first aid kit, water, chocolate, climbing gear, extra gloves and a warmer fleece in case the weather turns worse. The old fleece we found has been carried outside again. As it thawed, an awful smell spread in the hut, and it had to go.

At the foot of the small, icy slope rising up to the ridge, we are momentarily brought to a standstill by a crevasse. The procedure from yesterday is repeated, and after a few minutes we both stand on the other side of it. Besides two climbers traversing from Castor towards Breithorn and the Klein Matterhorn lift, we have seen no one. Because of the weather conditions effectively preventing rockfalls and avalanches, and, as there is no wind either, all we can hear is our footsteps on the frozen snow - and our heavy breathing, of course.

'Will you lead on the ice wall?' asks Brian as we approach the steep slope leading up towards the ridge.

'Sure, but I think I'm going to spend some time putting in protection,' I reply.

On my right, I find a crack in the rock where I can place a nut. A quickdraw is clipped into the nut and connects the protection with the rope. About halfway, I am running out of rope and yell to Brian that he can start climbing on running belay. Although the wall is relatively steep, it is within our comfort zone, for which reason I decide that we do not need to spend time on too many anchors.

After a short pitch of concentrated climbing, we reach the ridge. I try to see the route and to memorize special points in order to mark the route for the descent. I can easily imagine we will have to struggle when we get up higher where the rocks rising out of the snow are much taller than here. Brian takes off his crampons. Contrary to me, he prefers to climb in his boots when there is no snow on the rocks. There is a bit of wind at this altitude. It is not cold, but the wind is strong enough to remind us how changeable the mountain weather can be.

The first pitch is a mix of walking between big boulders on small paths and simple climbing. A lot of people would probably find this technically uninteresting, but we are having fun. At this point, we have already had to go back twice to find the route after having been led off. Again and again, Brian reads out loud from the guide book while we try to understand what the book is telling us.

Finally, we feel confident that we have found the right route and estimate another hour of climbing before we reach the summit.

'How do you feel about leaving the packs here to make an accelerated ascent?' I ask Brian.

'Fine by me! Just let me see if I can find somewhere to secure them safely,' he answers.

Using a sling, Brian ties our packs to a small tower, while I try to memorize what this spot looks like to make sure we can find it again, especially if it starts to snow while we are gone.

We leave the packs and continue to the right. Climbing without packs feels good despite them being lighter than usual. The guide book says something about fixed ropes on the most difficult parts, and right now we are searching for these ropes. We are facing a very steep wall, and I can hardly imagine crossing this section without some fixed equipment given the degree of difficulty it has in the guide book. However, since the tracks in the snow end here, I begin to think that we have – once again – lost the right track. Out comes the guidebook again.

'I really think we should have continued on the track we left before,' says Brian.

'But didn't the track come to a dead end there?' I ask.

'Yeah, sort of, but maybe we only needed to continue a few more meters to spot the fixed equipment,' he replies.

'Maybe; it's certainly worth a try.'

It is kind of amusing how we have developed this division of labor. Somehow it is always Brian who reads from the guidebook. Maybe because he is more patient than I am. However, he always asks for my opinion, and in that way we make a common decision and share the responsibility.

Neither of us feel too convinced that this is the right interpretation of the guide book, but if it is, there is no need to leave the packs here. We untie the sling and bring the packs along as we move further left towards the ridge.

'I see the fixed ropes!' Brian shouts and continues in a lower voice, 'if you can call that a rope'.

I rush up to him and immediately spot the long chain bolted to the rock.

'This is certainly exposed climbing,' I say with a smile as I look forward to getting started.

'You're right! Do you think this is the kind of route finding trouble we'll experience on the Matterhorn?' suggests Brian.

'Yes sir, times one hundred!' I reply.

'All right, take it away on the chains, Kjaer!' says Brian, and he continues mumbling that it looks like a pitch that I would enjoy more than him.

Actually, I think Brian and I climb at the same level, but every now and then we face a route or a pitch that is more appealing to one of us. This time, the challenge is to use our arms to pull ourselves up while balancing on small ledges on the rock face. Brian will, of course, have to climb the same pitch after me, but as the second he will be climbing with a tight rope being belayed by me from up above. The mental pressure of climbing second is therefore not as great.

We agree to leave the backpacks here and keep our fingers crossed that we will not need any of their contents. This decision makes a lot of sense even though we are aware that we jeopardize some of the safety buffers in our climbing. In this situation, however, the argument that 'speed equals safety' wins.

I realize that I am going to need a couple of quickdraws and ask Brian to give me his. I use my left hand to grip the chain while the right one is used to clip the quickdraw into the bolt above my head, that locks the chain to the rock. The rope is clipped into the other end of the quickdraw. Brian takes in rope, and I am now on belay and start climbing. Beside the fact that fixed ropes add a lot of safety to your climbing, they are also a reliable signpost. It surely feels good to know that we are on the right track now. I traverse a couple of meters and begin to climb the steep chimney leading up to the last vertical face. The chimney is narrow enough for me to bridge between its walls. With a foot on each wall, I rest all my body weight on my feet, and in that way I can stand comfortably. It is quite a different matter when I have to move a foot, because every time I do so, the pressure on the remaining foot is changed and the balance is shifted.

'Don't do the splits!' Brian says cheerfully while I struggle to make my moves look just a little graceful.

I acknowledge the warning and do my best not to get stuck. I push on and mobilize all my concentration in order not to slip. The last piece of protection is a couple of meters behind me, and a fall from here would not be good for my pretty face. I finally reach the wall, and to my relief I find a shelf wide enough for me to stand relaxed with both feet placed on horizontal rock. On my harness, I always carry a short sling with a carabiner with which I quickly clip into the last bolt.

'I'm safe! You can take me out!' I shout to Brian.

'OK! You're out!'

I pull in the rope until it jams in a crack. Brian shouts and instructs me to give some slack so that he can free it.

Brian and I pull at the rope in turn until it comes free, and he can start climbing.

After having climbed together with Brian for many years, I know when to make a funny comment and when to keep my big mouth shut – or at least I should know. I suppose that I, every now and then, misjudge the situation. In this particular situation, it would probably have been a better choice to have let Brian climb in peace rather than to talk about the weather, the Irishmen and their return to Zermatt and our plans for tomorrow. It is not that Brian specifically tells me to shut up, but the look on his face ought to make me realize that it is time for me to mind my own business. Even if Brian is now exactly at the point where I was minutes ago when I had to listen to his smart comments, I decide to better hold my tongue. I can see that he is concentrating hard. He will soon find his rhythm, I think. Afterwards he will surely say, 'Gees, Kjaer, well done!' I will then proceed to thank him for his kind words, and we will end up in the usual nerdy discussion about the mental difference between climbing first and second. Just like all the other times we have had the discussion, we will conclude that the second would probably also have been able to lead the pitch had he been the first.

The final pitch on the steep wall is quite easy as the chains have been mounted alongside good foot placements, and it is easy to find spots for additional protection. It only takes a few minutes before I reach the snow at the end of the wall, and from here, I belay Brian as he climbs up to me.

Standing here in the snow, we can almost see the summit. Well, at least for a short while before the clouds close in again. A giant Madonna statue is posing a few meters behind us. These statues and different kinds of crosses are something one meets a lot in the mountains. There must be an explanation for this, and I make a mental note of investigating this phenomenon before we head back home. I am convinced that it must take some good arguments to make somebody build a concrete base on which to place a bronze figure weighing several hundred kilos, in such a remote place!

The next section is pure joy for Brian as he leads along the last semi-steep ridge leading directly to the summit. It is hard work, but Brian soon finds a good pace, and his machine-like rhythm of placing his axe up high on the ridge, moving his left foot, then his right, then releasing and replacing the axe and so on, quickly eats up meter by meter. Brian has taken part in many sporting disciplines, and he has the habit of measuring pleasure in sweat and muscle soreness. I feel confident that he is enjoying today's climb, and I know that he is experienced enough to pace himself all the way to the summit.

'Steffen, I have to cross a not-to-good looking crevasse; you'll have to belay me when I cross it!' shouts Brian.

'No worries, I'll place some protection. Hang on!' I reply.

First, I try to place a snow anchor, but I realize that the snow is much too hard. It is too soft, however, for an ice screw, so I end up placing my axe deep enough to use it as protection to belay Brian. Because of the clouds, the visibility on the mountain is reduced to about half the distance between us, and, consequently, I cannot see the crevasse myself. I wonder, though, why we run into a crevasse with the ridge only a few meters away. Given this short distance, I doubt Brian will try to jump across the crevasse; it would be too risky.

'On belay!' I shout and await his instructions about how he is going to cross.

'OK, climbing!' he yells back.

Soon the rope starts moving. Slowly, but steady. No sudden pulls and no jerks. All I can see is the rope, the snow around me and the broken cornice a few meters to my right. I know the mountain face beyond the cornice is vertical and probably continues like that all the way down to the glacier far below. Yet, I feel safe. On a good day, visibility would seem infinite from here, maybe 50 kilometers or more, but all I have is five meters!

'OK, you're on belay now, but wait for my signal!' Brian commands.

I can hear his axe working overtime and know that he will soon clip his harness sling into it, put the rope in his belay device and tell me to start climbing.

The crevasse is about one meter wide, and I can easily understand why Brian did not trust it. I can see the marks from his crampons and axe placements and try to decide which foot to place on the small snow tower standing precariously in the middle of the crevasse. I inform Brian that I am climbing and step onto the edge of the crevasse. From here, I am supposed to step out onto the snow tower and, in the same movement, reach across the crevasse and hammer my axe into the other side. Now it is my turn to compliment the lead climber, but all in due time. I take a swing with the axe; it is a perfect hit, which is fortunate since, at that very moment, a big chunk of the tower breaks off and disappears down into the depths of the crevasse. I use the axe to pull myself up and meet Brian with the deepest respect for what he has just done.

'Are we ready for the last 100 meters?' he asks and starts climbing.

Sitting on the summit, we enjoy the moment even though we can feel the cold creeping in on us. Facing away from the ridge, we compliment ourselves for a good day's work while staring into the air – or, rather, into the cloud. Brian is counting silently and concludes that this was mountain number three with no view, and then proceeds to explain the statistical probabilities for improvement on mountain number four.

We are in no hurry to begin the descent, so we spend some time eating chocolate and discussing the climb. I am quite enthusiastic and believe this mountain to be a new favorite. It is definitely a good training ground for our coming Matterhorn experience. All the trouble finding the right route and the challenges on the fixed rope and chains make perfect mental acclimatization for the Matterhorn where we expect to find exactly these hurdles, only in much larger quantities. Surely the Matterhorn will also offer us a labyrinth of loose rocks and lots of opportunities to swear at the too brief descriptions in the guide book.

Despite little wind, the cold now forces us to get going again. It is time to get back down. We remind each other not to lose concentration and that the descent is often the most dangerous part: after a strenuous climb, one is inclined to feel that the goal is met with the inevitable effect that concentration is reduced. This is documented by too many sad stories from the mountains.

'Looks like we've got more company,' I say to Brian, as we approach the hut.

In front of the hut, there is a man cleaning his pan. We greet him with a polite 'hello' and get a German greeting in return. Inside we salute a lady, who is kind enough to pretend not to be disturbed by us. We ask about their plans but soon realize that conversation is a bit tough. They only know a few words of English, and our German is quite poor. They point out on the map where they have been and where they want to go. We point out the mountains we have climbed, smile and nod!

'Phil has sent a text message,' I almost shout to Brian.

'What does he say?'

'He says that the weather forecast is perfect from Saturday and the following four days, and that the certainty of the forecast is really high...how about it, partner?' I ask with my eyes wide with excitement.

'Are you sure?'

'Yes!'

For a moment, the situation is about to get out of hand. Brian reacts to the good news by offering double portions for dinner while I rush through my clothes to find some candy. This calls for celebration! I declare.

'What shall I reply?' I ask.

'Tell them there is free beer at The Brown Cow on Friday night,' Brian answers as he uses his fingers to count the days.

'So what about Castor? Should we still give it a go tomorrow?' he asks.

'Sure! If the weather allows it, that would be a great mountain to tick off,' I answer.

‘If we leave early and take all our stuff and leave it at the foot of the mountain, I assume we can make it back to the lift before it closes down for the day. In that way, we’ll be back in Zermatt tomorrow night,’ concludes Brian.

We forget about everything else and start planning the details for the next couple of days. We decide to rest on Saturday, hike up to the Hörnli Hut at the foot of the Matterhorn on Sunday, and so Monday will be the day for the big battle!

Poor Matterhorn

Few mountains have had to put up with as many experiments or crazy ideas as the Matterhorn. Engineers have competed in hatching one insane plan after the other, many companies have tried everything to link their products to the Matterhorn, and many more or less thoroughly considered projects have been initiated by less than competent climbers on the mountain.

On a good day, the view from the Matterhorn extends all the way to Mont Blanc, and if the engineers a hundred years ago had had their way, we would have been able to ride a train up both of these mountains. Whereas they actually built the first part of the tramway up to 2372 meters on Mont Blanc, the plans for the Matterhorn did not make it past the engineers' drawing table. These were ambitious plans, and had they been carried through, tourists today would be able to ascend the mountain by train, by gondola or – even crazier – by elevator, deep inside the mountain.

Ever since the spectacular first successful ascent of the Matterhorn in 1865, the commercialization of the mountain has been steadily increasing and the publicity efforts enormous. The best example may be the Swiss chocolate bar, Toblerone, which, by its shape and the print on the packaging, is unambiguously associated with the Matterhorn.

To others, the fascinating Matterhorn has been the inspiration for crazy stunts such as the idea of covering part of the mountain in chains of lights, or having a newspaper stand flown up on the ridge to surprise a friend.

In the mountaineering world, there is a lot of talk about ethics, and to most climbers a pure and discrete ascent is an important part of the goal. To others, it is part of the game to test or challenge what is possible. And Poor Matterhorn; one thing is to put up with the uncountable numbers of climbers and the exclamations of joy from those who make it to the summit. Another thing is to put up with violin or brass music, golfers who want to tee out to every corner of the world, parachutists and skiers who construct ramps for take-off, film crews shooting more or less serious movies, and climbers from all over the world, who just want to leave a personal something on the mountain or find a small rock to take home. All of this happens on the summit of the beautiful Matterhorn.

The Visitor's Book

IV

A Tragedy

We were five people doing the Hörnli Ridge - two Germans, one Spaniard and us two Scots. There was lots of snow and we were slow. We left the hut at 3:45 am, and at 12:15 pm, just below the fixed ropes to the summit, we had to turn back, tired. One of the Germans then went missing, and we all went to the Solvay Hut and called for help. From there we began abseiling, and the Spaniard - Mariano - slipped, and unroped he fell down the east face. The other German and the two of us then abseiled, slowly and cautiously, down to the Hörnli Hut arriving there at 1 am. The bodies of the German, Marcus, and the Spaniard, Mariano, were both found by the search helicopters. The message is to be very, very careful!

Alan & Alan, Scotland
July 17th, 2001

A Tough Decision

Friday, July 4th

Beep beep...beep beep!

It is 5.30 am and it is a bloody cold morning, to say the least. From the bunk bed I can see through the window: the day is still dawning and looks everything but inviting. A morning like this at 3750 meters can be absolutely stunning, and if you have witnessed just one sunrise in the mountains, you become addicted. On the other hand, when the mountains are covered in dense clouds, the pleasure is severely limited – as is the case today!

I am still in my sleeping bag trying to savor all the warmth before the inevitable: I must get up. I pull down my cap, knitted, woolen and warm, to cover my ears, and I wrestle with the numerous blankets I have managed to wrap around myself during the night. My guess is that the temperature in the hut is close to zero, and it is very tempting to stay in the bag under the blankets for another couple of hours.

'Don't you think you should check the weather, Kjaer?' mumbles Brian.

'Nope, it's your job today!'

'Well, I think we need to send a specialist – you go,' he says before diving deep down into his sleeping bag, from where I can detect utterances about how highly he regards my skills in meteorology.

'Right...I'll give you the weather report from here: it is freezing, no visibility, and the wind looks moderate.'

'Don't you think it would be better to actually check the weather,' the talking sleeping bag continues.

Sometimes I am just too easy. In order to avoid being accused of whining in the cold conditions, I give up.

From the door, I can confirm my predictions. Brian continues and suggests that I might as well melt some snow and prepare breakfast now that I am up, allowing him to stay in bed and save his energy for the big climb.

It is the speed of our stove melting snow that dictates the pace this morning. The first round of water is used for breakfast and coffee. Round two enables us to take several liters of drinking water with us on the climb up Castor. The process of getting water is still quite burdensome as we have not managed to find any new snow around the hut. Consequently, we have to boil the water for an extended period of time and then filter it afterwards.

The Germans are also up now. They are quietly packing for their planned excursion. They do not talk much, but I think they are enjoying mountain life. We, on the other hand, talk a lot! At the center of our current discussion is the question of what route to take on Castor. In many ways, the mountain reminds us of Mont Blanc du Tacul, which we have climbed three times before: a long steep walk on packed snow with difficult passages across numerous crevasses. Well, at least this is what we assume as we prepare for a long day, during which we are not only going to climb Castor, but also intend to make it all the way back to Klein Matterhorn to catch the lift down to Zermatt.

Although we have now eaten most of our food rations, the packs are still heavy to carry as we climb down the rocks from the hut. We are fully focused – carefully placing our feet and searching for something to hold on to. I am cold and I look forward to reaching the track on the snow on which we will be able to walk fast enough to work up some heat.

We soon cross the ice wall and reach the snow plateau, and as we approach Pollux, I think about the days we have had up here. I think we have made the best of it: we have had excellent altitude exposure with three ascents above 4000 meters, and I am absolutely sure we are well prepared for the Matterhorn.

Below the southwest face of Pollux, we decide to leave the packs behind. Given our tight schedule, being freed from the weight on our shoulders will greatly increase our chance of making it to the summit of Castor in time. Since we will return along the same track, this is a suitable place to leave the gear. The terrain is sloping, and since the wind is picking up, we decide to secure the packs to the ice below: with my axe, I scrape away the snow and place an ice screw. Meanwhile, Brian is sorting our gear and supplies. I connect the ice screw with a carabiner to the packs, and I make sure to place them in a way that allows the bright orange and yellow colors to be visible from different angles and from some distance.

Brian informs me that he has chosen a chocolate bar for each of us, along with two bottles of water and a first aid kit. We fill our pockets and head towards Castor.

We turn the corner below Pollux and are met by a strong wind that I had not noticed earlier today. Visibility is fine at this altitude, but from where we are now, I can see that the upper half of Castor is covered in swiftly-moving clouds. I tell Brian that I find it a bit too much to struggle, not only with route finding, but also with crevasses and strong winds.

Brian shares my concern, and we pause to evaluate the situation. The choice is between canceling the attempt on Castor and starting the climb, hoping that the weather improves within the next couple of hours. We decide to give it a go since the first part of the mountain does not seem too steep, and since we will always be able to turn back.

I am freezing, and I bitterly regret that I did not put on an extra layer. I convince myself that I will be able to work up some body heat when the climbing becomes steeper. The doubt is there, though. It had been okay to climb Central Summit, Roccia Nera and Pollux with little or no visibility, but then we did not have the wind to contend with. I tell Brian that I am willing to give it 15 more minutes. If I have not gotten any warmer by then, I want us to turn back. Apparently, Brian has no problems keeping warm, but he is, of course, ready to call it quits if I ask him to – that is part of the deal.

Still, it is a hard decision. The mountain is right there, just waiting to be climbed. Fortunately, we always try to make our decisions based on rational, rather than emotional, considerations. We are always prepared to stop and turn back should the conditions be too dangerous, or if we do not feel fit to master both the ascent and descent safely.

On the mountain, the clouds are racing by. I am fascinated by the scenery. The light is shifting constantly, and time and again, the colors change to produce yet another image. There is nothing left to discuss, though. I am freezing, and there is nothing to suggest that warmth will return on this cold mountain. I explain my situation to Brian, and we decide to turn back. It is an easy decision. From here, it will take us about 45 minutes back to the packs, and I cannot wait to pull out my spare fleece.

As we pass Pollux, we are surprised by a clear view to the summit of Roccia Nera. It may not be the biggest mountain in the world, but it sure looks impressive with its steep rock walls. I think back and remember how we fumbled around looking for the right route. It seems like we have left the bad weather behind Pollux. The weather improves as we increase our distance to Castor. It is now quite pleasant, I think, and Brian must have the same perception as he suggests that we climb the main summit of Breithorn on the way home. Even though I feel a bit knackered, I am easily talked into the project. If we can keep up the pace, we should be able to make it to the foot of the Breithorn in an hour, and from there it should only take us another hour to the summit.

I look forward to getting the weight of the pack off my shoulders once again. Normally this is not a concern, but the extended period of time in the mountains has taken its toll. I feel that my body needs rest. It will do us good with a day of restitution tomorrow – especially at only 1620 meters in Zermatt.

Our track across the glacier is clearly visible. Many crevasses are hidden below snow bridges, although most of them reveal themselves as the heat from the sun has caused the snow to melt and sag thus leaving clues as to where the crevasses lie. Snow bridges are treacherous. We know this from experience. On a hot day, they may collapse from even the smallest additional load, whereas even thin bridges can be very strong in freezing conditions.

As we pass a snow bridge, the surface breaks and suddenly collapses under me. One of my legs goes into the crevasse, and there I am – hanging with an arm on either side of it.

Behind me, Brian has thrown his entire weight on his axe. This is exactly how we have practiced it: by doing so, he will be able to brake my fall should I continue down into the crevasse. We have the situation under control, but it does not change the seriousness of the incident. I am annoyed with myself. Why did I not see the crevasse? I know my carelessness could have caused an accident. An accident that could ultimately have been fatal for both of us, should I have dragged Brian down into the crevasse after me. On the other hand, we both reacted the way we were supposed to: I did what I could to stop the fall with my arms and axe, and Brian acted promptly to break the fall. I express my gratitude to Brian, and I promise to be more careful.

The incident is a perfect example of the potential dangers surrounding us, and it reminds us that climbing and mountaineering demand constant concentration.

The traffic up and down Breithorn is not as heavy as the last time we were here, although there are still around ten people coming down and several more going up. What a highway!

It has been almost four hours since we left the hut, and even if we have paused from time to time to discuss what to do next, we have not had much to eat and drink. Refueling is therefore our number one priority before starting the ascent of the Breithorn. We sit down on the packs and allow ourselves a short break before proceeding. Scattered snowflakes are falling slowly and silently. There is hardly any wind. It is amazing how big the difference in the weather can be over a short distance: the distance between Castor and Breithorn is only about four kilometers, and whereas it was almost storm-like on Castor, there is not a breath of wind on the Breithorn.

I drink about half a liter of water, eat some chocolate and a muesli bar and hope that the sugar will boost my energy levels.

'How long do you think it will take us to the top?' asks Brian.

'About one hour. I am a bit tired, but this is where we should feel our acclimatization kick in...'

'Don't you think we can do it faster?' Brian continues.

'Let's try!'

I can already feel how the water and food have done wonders, and I look forward to this short climb. In five days, we will then have managed to cross the 4000 meter line four times. Not bad at all and perfect acclimatization for the Matterhorn.

An ascent of the Breithorn is a straightforward climb, and this peak is actually known as the easiest 4000'er in the Alps. Still, you need to think, concentrate and be careful. This is an alpine route, and a visit to the graveyard by the village church reveals many tombstones telling sad stories from the Breithorn. Unfortunately, many have the idea that the Breithorn is an effortless run up and down, and on our way we meet several people without crampons or axes. If they are unable to break a slip or fall on these snow fields, they expose themselves to severe danger.

Normally, Brian would lead on a route like this allowing us to take advantage of his physique. This time, however, he is behind me, and I am now determined to shake him off; quite a task considering that we are roped together! Although we normally never compete amongst ourselves while climbing, this is a good opportunity to test our acclimatization – and to test my physical shape.

Since the route is easy and constantly sloping, I am quickly able to find a good rhythm. Every now and then, I try to increase the pace a bit to work as close as possible to my threshold. This is mainly to test the effect of our training and the recent preparation in the mountains, but also to see if we can actually do the climb faster than the estimated one hour.

After 44 minutes we reach the summit. There is hardly any wind and – of course – no view! Ten minutes before we got here, a giant cloud decided to position itself on the upper reaches of the mountain. Regrettably, there is nothing to indicate that it is going to move.

'What about a summit photo?' laughs Brian.

'Of course,' I reply, 'and when we return back home we can shape the stories as we wish.' I smile at the thought of the many identical summit shots all bearing the same title: Brian and Steffen in the clouds.

The lack of view, however, does not diminish our satisfaction: in five days we have climbed four mountains all higher than 4000 meters. We certainly feel prepared for the primary objective of this trip: the Matterhorn!

The Mountain Guide

The mountain guide Andreas Perren (born 1968) is, with his more than 100 trips on the Matterhorn, one of the most experienced guides in Zermatt. Many years ago, it was Andreas' great-grandfather who guided on the Matterhorn. 'Back then the money was made on the mountain. One day's work on the Matterhorn would pay the same as 30 days of work in the village. It is not like that anymore,' Andreas adds with a smile.

Andreas talks about the strategies he uses when he guides his clients on the Matterhorn:'To me, it's important that we are at the front of the pack when the long line of mountaineers leave the hut in the morning. In that way we can minimize the waiting time near the difficult passages, and thereby I seek to avoid breaking the rhythm in my client's climbing.'

Andreas says that he has a clear impression of the abilities of his clients and their chances of making it all the way to the summit after only 50 meters. Like other guides, he works with a fixed, predetermined time frame for the climb: he wants to reach the Solvay Hut no later than three hours after leaving the Hörnli Hut. This rule is in agreement with the statistics stating that 80 to 90% of all accidents happen in the afternoon: after many hours on the mountain under a baking sun, the often unfit clients are exhausted, and, furthermore, the sun has melted the snow and ice that prevents rocks from falling.

Living at the foot of the Matterhorn naturally leaves you with a profound knowledge about the history of the mountain. Perhaps this is why Andreas is so put off by the changing ethics related to climbing the Matterhorn. Whereas people used to respect the Solvay Hut as an emergency hut, it is Andreas' impression that more and more people use it as free lodgings and in that way extend the climb over two or even three days. 'Only a few years ago, it was unheard of to use the hut like that. Unfortunately, the Matterhorn has now become a 24 hour mountain, and I actually think that it would be a good idea to remove the Solvay Hut as it would discourage the most inexperienced from trying to climb the mountain,' says Andreas.

Whether Andreas' colleagues share his opinion remains unknown. The solidarity between the guides is, he believes, much improved now compared to earlier. '20 or 30 years ago, the guides kept in small tightly knit groups when spending nights in the huts. Back then it was a family business. Today it is different. Now everybody talks with everybody,' says Andreas.

In his experience, also the working conditions for guides on the Matterhorn have been significantly improved since the rules were changed in 2002. It is now required that inexperienced clients have practiced and acclimatized with a guide on other mountains before being allowed to give the Matterhorn a go. In that way, the guide is able to assess the skill and fitness level of his client on less dangerous ground. Andreas informs me that whereas the success rate used to be 60 percent, it is now 90 to 95 percent of the clients who make it all the way to the summit.

Andreas Perren is pleased with the many friendships he has acquired in the mountains, and he is satisfied with the fact that he, after so many years on the Matterhorn, is still able to smile when he stands in Zermatt and looks up on the mountain.

The Visitor's Book

V

A Dream Fulfilled

Three months of dreaming has come to an end! Finally, yesterday, July 27th, the three of us stood at the top of the Matterhorn. We reached the summit at 11am after a 7 hour ascent. The weather was perfect, and the feeling of being on the top of the Matterhorn was unbeatable. Regrettably, the descent took way too long. Due to queues by the fixed ropes we were prevented from making it back to the Hörnli Hut before nightfall. Just in case, we decided to wait for daylight and spent the rest of the night in a couloir. The night was wonderful but bitterly cold. By 4 am we could see the lights from climbers coming up from the hut. As daylight came we continued our descent to the Hörnli. A dream fulfilled!

Bjarke, Ketil and Aksel, Norway
July 28th, 2002

Final Preparations

Saturday, July 5th

Normally, the joy of expectation will dwarf everything else before a climb, but with the Matterhorn it is not quite like that: I am both fascinated and frightened by this magnificent mountain. The joy is there, but most of all I think I'm excited. The proportions of the mountain are just as enormous as I expect the challenges of climbing it will be. Many thoughts are filling my head. From the campsite I can see most of the mountain which, with its strange isolated position, shoots up into the sky. Amazing! Had anyone asked me to draw the perfect mountain, it would have looked like the Matterhorn. Will we make it? I am firmly convinced that we are fit and acclimatized, and I have no doubts that our climbing skills are adequate. It is the route-finding difficulties that bother me most. I therefore consider spending the afternoon in the bookshop to scan through the voluminous collection of Matterhorn books. In that way I hope to learn more about the route and perhaps even be able to recognize it when we are on the mountain.

I tell Brian that I think I will spend some time in the book shop looking at photos of the Matterhorn, and I reveal my thoughts and speculations concerning the climb.

'Probably a good idea, but perhaps we should make a list of all the other things we also need to do?' he suggests.

We are sitting in front of the tent and enjoying our breakfast. Brian is already writing a 'to-do list', while I am reading the recommendations given in the guide book. This process serves a mental as well as a practical purpose, and as my knowledge about the mountain and the chosen route grows, I am overwhelmed by enthusiasm.

The weather is awesome. The sun is shining from a clear blue sky, and the anticipation of a full day's rest is certainly making this a perfect morning. We have, of course, arranged the chairs and table so that we can both enjoy the view of the Matterhorn.

On the gravel road behind the campsite, a man is busy cordoning off the area to prepare for a mountain marathon. Paragliders are floating above us trying to read the winds in order to make soft landings on the grass next to the railway line. We are actually in the middle of everything, and we did not even intend to be. Perfect! The endless points on the to-do list are ignored as we agree to spend some hours around camp. Brian is keen on watching the race, and I will play with my photo gear and maybe shoot some photos of the runners as they pass by.

For a number of years, photography has been one of my major interests. At first, the objective was to capture the impressions from canoe trips in Sweden. Most of the pictures showed an unspoiled wilderness, were portraits of travel partners or the simple camp life. Unfortunately, the photos also told the story of my poor photographic skills and mediocre equipment. Too often I returned from the photo shop with blurred photos that did no justice to the scenery or the memorable moments. Perhaps that is why I quit photography for a while. In 1999, however, I participated in an alpine course at Kebnekaise in Sweden, and my inner photographer was reawakened. I was immensely fascinated by the magnitude and colors of the mountain landscape, and I sensed a sincere thrill when I, in the hunt for the right angle and the perfect shot, experienced nature in a completely new way. All of a sudden, I did not just see the track in front of me and all the other immediate impressions; I had found meaning in the otherwise tiring hike into the mountains. It may actually have been at this point I realized that the process is just as important as the goal.

'Have you seen the small camera?' I ask Brian, who is busy repairing his crampons.

'Nope, but right now I'm so furious that I can't see straight!' he explains while he struggles with wire and pliers to fix his crampons, which were damaged on the rocks of the Pollux.

'Let me do it!'

'Thanks, but I really ought to do it myself,' he says and continues to curse the manufacturer.

Under the crampons we have mounted plates of rubber to prevent the snow from clogging under the boots, but the material is too fragile to withstand mixed climbing. When we first got the crampons, we changed the anti-balling plates every time they broke, but we soon learned that this was too expensive. Instead, we now repair them as well as we can.

'If you don't mind, you can finish this...the alternative is that I'll buy a new pair. I really don't understand why they use such crappy materials,' Brian says.

'OK, let me try. By the way, I have been thinking about which style to use on the Matterhorn. I know we have planned to take the tent, sleeping bags and stove, and sleep somewhere near the Hörnli Hut, but I think we would benefit from a slightly different approach.'

'What do you mean?' asks Brian.

'I think we should devote all our efforts to the climb and forget everything about digging out a spot for the tent, melting snow and all that. I suggest we book two beds in the Hörnli Hut, buy the food and in that way buy ourselves the time and energy to explore the first part of the route in daylight!'

'You may be right, but do you think we can get beds at the hut with such short notice?'

'It is worth a try, but what do you think about the idea?' I ask.

'I think it's a good idea. Let's give them a call...we can find the number in the guide book.'

Despite the difficulties with repairing the crampons, I actually enjoy the struggle. Countless times before, I have dismantled various sorts of equipment just to learn how it works. I have now sharpened the axes to make them bite perfectly: it brings me a certain satisfaction to fix my own gear and to know that I will be able to repair it "in action" should it be necessary. At home, I am unable to manage even the simplest repairs on my car. I am far from being a handyman, but with my climbing equipment it is different.

As soon as Brian finds the phone number to the hut, I call them. The guardian informs me that there is plenty of room and that he does not expect too many climbers as it is still early season. Absolutely perfect! I book two beds and ask him about arrival and departure times.

'The guardian said that dinner is served at 6 pm so we just have to arrive before that. He also said that everyone is woken up at 3.30 am,' I tell Brian.

'Super!'

It feels as if we, by this maneuver, have come a lot closer to the mountain. The part of the planning that has to do with drinking water, cooking, and tenting is now irrelevant, and we can focus solely on the climb.

Much to my own irritation, I realize that I have exposed my shoulders to the sun for too long. It is not going to be any fun with a heavy backpack on them, and I curse my own stupidity. It is hard, though, not to be seduced by the excellent weather. I have been preoccupied with taking pictures and checking our gear and not given the strong sun a single thought.

Our equipment is scattered on a large area around the tent. Every now and then, Brian gets up and moves the piles a bit to signal to the other campers that there is still room for them. We are sorting clothes and gear for tomorrow's attempt on the Matterhorn – and this time we try to be tough; we are not carrying anything that will not be needed. On the other hand, we are not leaving anything behind that could increase safety on the mountain.

We each make a pile of personal gear. In my pile I place clothes, boots, crampons, axe, camera and water bottles. We also have a common pile of climbing gear, which we have so far managed to keep down to one rope, four camming devices, some nuts and quickdraws, two ice screws and a snow anchor. We also need to reduce our bulky first aid kit and decide which guide book to take. Together with map and compass, this book is what we have to rely on when we face problems finding the right way.

In the center of the campsite, Peter, Phil and Mark are busy trying to identify the perfect position for their binoculars, which are mounted on a tripod and directed towards the Matterhorn. I ask them what they are doing, and Phil explains that he is tuning his gear to prepare for a close monitoring of our attempt from the campsite. I am touched; I have never felt such sincere interest from other climbers. Mark asks about our plans, and I explain our recent decision about changing the approach. I can tell they like the decision – in fact they almost seem relieved. I fail to understand why and ask Mark how he is feeling. He still feels dehydrated and weak after the night in the Rossi Volante Hut, and they have therefore decided to postpone other adventures for a couple of days.

I spend the better part of the afternoon in the bookstore searching through many books. I have a particular interest in coffee-table books. One of them describes the climbers' route to the summit, image by image. I am completely absorbed by the book, which conveys the story of a successful climb with more than a hundred color photos. For the first time, I see the long, sturdy fixed ropes, close-ups of the Solvay Hut at 4003 meters and the endless line of boulders and towers on the ridge. Photo by photo, I am taken through the many meters of altitude that must be climbed before one can celebrate on the summit. I soon realize that the book is of limited value in terms of learning the route in detail. Nevertheless, it has great value for my mental preparation. It yields good insight into the technical challenges we will meet, and it gives me an overview of the different stages of the climb. The final photos are taken from a helicopter and show a small group of cheering mountaineers on the summit of the Matterhorn. I want to go there, I think, and feel convinced that we will succeed!

It is as if the many thoughts I had about the Matterhorn back home do not match the current image in my head. Even if I thought we had investigated every aspect, I keep finding new details, and it all contributes to my ever growing interest in the mountain. Back home, it was merely a dream about a climb and the more technical questions related to that, but now it is so much more. Living here, close to the mountain, and looking at it every day has changed my perspective. I imagine what it must have been like in those hectic days around the first successful ascent in 1865, and I admire the men that stubbornly kept trying because they firmly believed that it was possible. I now know the sad story and their destiny; I have seen their tombstones in the graveyard. I have read the legends and understood the immense importance this mountain has for this area. I have also realized that the Matterhorn is so much more than just another mountain.

'There's a movie in the local cinema tonight about Zermatt and the Matterhorn – do you want to come along and watch it,' I ask Brian when we meet at the supermarket.

'Is it about climbing the mountain?' he asks.

'Err...well...that I don't know, but I met the manager of the Alpine Museum, and he told me it was really good!'

'I suppose it's part of his job to say that, isn't it?'

'Maybe, but what's there to lose? We could meet up with the Irishmen at the pub afterwards?' I plead.

'All right!'

Besides meat and parmesan cheese for yet another pasta dish, we also need to buy something to bring on the climb. I was thinking along the lines of chocolate and biscuits, but Brian has found some small cakes for which he guarantees the nutritional value. I am talked into leaving the biscuits. A bar of chocolate and two cakes each will have to do.

While Brian is preparing dinner, I pack the most necessary first aid gear. I bring plasters, cleansing tissues, a compress, bandages, a selection of pills – both ordinary painkillers, pills for acute diarrhea, and something stronger that will be able to ease the pain should one of us suffer a fracture. I inform Brian about the contents to make sure that both of us will be able to find what is needed in case of emergency.

We discuss which guide book to bring. Brian suggests Selected Climbs by Lindsay Griffin. He thinks it contains more details. I pack the book, the map and the compass in the top pocket of my backpack. We have decided to leave tomorrow morning at about

10 am and estimate arriving at the Hörnli Hut at about 1 pm. The rest of the afternoon will then be available for thoroughly exploring the first part of the route. We plan to climb the first couple of hundred meters to make it easier to find the route in the dark morning hours on the following day.

As we eat, I think about how pleased I am with what we have achieved today even though it has all been in the town rather than in the mountains. After some strenuous days, it has been really nice to take it easy. It also feels good that we have checked all the details. The sun has already set behind the mountains, leaving the valley in shadow. Still I cannot help but take another look at the Matterhorn and yet again I am fascinated.

'I'm sure we are going to make it!' I say to Brian

Something has gathered a crowd at the Irishmen's tent. On our way to the cinema we stop to see what is going on. In the middle of it all sits the winner of the mountain marathon, and it does not take me long to learn that such an accomplishment creates cock-and-bull stories in the same manner as climbing mountains does. We congratulate the winner while Peter signals to us that they have tried to get rid of the crowd for some time now. We agree to meet them at The Brown Cow after the movie and hurry on to the cinema.

The spirits are high at the small table. Mark teaches us that beer must be bought in pitchers and drunk before the foam settles. He is on top, and it certainly seems as if he has recovered from his altitude problems. He is not completely well, he says, but as far as he is concerned, a visit to the pub has always been the best medicine back in Ireland, and he rests assured that it will work in Switzerland too. Phil asks about the movie and Brian explains, in a slightly disappointed manner, how it was all about the tough life of the mountain farmers.

We do not agree completely, Brian and I, about the value of the movie. I found it quite entertaining, but I must admit that even if the hardship of the farmers was always illustrated with the Matterhorn in the background, it did not bring us much new knowledge relevant for the climb. Luckily, Brian's disappointment is swiftly and quickly flushed away in the cheerful company.

Peter tells us that he and Phil have decided to visit us at the Hörnli Hut tomorrow afternoon. They plan to start early and walk all the way from Zermatt. I am impressed! It means 1600 meters of ascent on steep gravel tracks – and all that just to see us well on the way. I sense that our ascent means a lot to them, and I am sincerely happy for their support. Phil keeps repeating that he will follow us from the camp, and that he knows we are strong enough, and that we have the right attitude for this game.

'I'm quite taken by their interest,' I say to Brian as we lie in the tent.

'Yeah I know, it's fantastic...almost overwhelming,' he replies.

'We should probably buy them a beer when we get back down!'

'I wouldn't be surprised if they won't let us...I think they'll insist on paying!'

'You're probably right,' I answer and ask if he can think of anything we have forgotten?

'No, but what do we do with the tent? Should we just leave it here or what?'

'Why not? It's just for one night. We'll be back Monday night, and by then I'm sure we'll appreciate not having to trouble ourselves with putting up a tent!'

'By the way, I checked the weather forecast on the way down to the pub. It's perfect, not a single cloud for the next four days.'

'I know, I saw it too. Someone powerful up above must be on our side, don't you think?'

'Absolutely! Goodnight!'

'Goodnight!'

Glaciers Shaped the Matterhorn

What is more credible? That the majestic Matterhorn got its shape by mere chance or that it is the result of millions of years of wear and tear from the harsh climate? It must be up to the individual to decide.

The Alps were formed around 90 million years ago when Africa came so close to Europe that a collision between the gigantic tectonic plates caused the terrain to rise. A mountain chain was created. Since then, glaciers have eroded the mountains. The glaciers have been much bigger than they are now, and they were all created during periods with more snow falling than melting. In places where the terrain was not level, the glaciers were pulled downwards by gravity, and in this process, the enormous masses of ice polished the mountain faces bit by bit. The characteristic shape of the Matterhorn is thus caused by glaciers polishing its four sides through millions of years. If someone finds this explanation a bit dubious, they may choose to believe the story about God who, on one of his many trips around the world inspecting his work, passed by the Alps. One day he was in Zermatt, and as he crossed the Theodul Pass, his cane got stuck in the rocks; even though he shook it from side to side, it did not come loose. Only when he put all his might into it, the cane broke and the lower part remained stuck in the rock. God went on, and when he turned around to look at the part of the cane still stuck in the rock, he saw what we today call the Matterhorn.

The Visitor's Book
VI

Status: 12 Dead

It's nearly the end of the season, and as I'm sitting in The North Wall Bar, I have decided to write in this book.

My name is Jodie and I work at the Hörnli Hut. From reading some of the things in our guestbook, or this one here, I have to state that I have seen 12 deaths this season, which is fewer than normal. We deal with this every year, so if you don't have a guide, make sure you're experienced and listen to the weather reports, then you can go and enjoy it!

Jodie, hut assistant, Hörnli Hut
September 6th, 2001

Towards the Matterhorn

Sunday, July 6th

I can hear Brian clattering with the pans outside the tent. It's just past 8 am, and the characteristic noises from the railway blend in with the noise from Brian's activity. I am still in my sleeping bag, and as I am slowly waking up, I think about the climb: tomorrow at this time, we will already be far up the Matterhorn. I am looking forward to it. I can hear that Brian has got the stove going now, which signals coffee within the next five minutes – hopefully served in bed! I think about last week. It has exceeded my expectations. The weather could have been better, but it has been good enough for us to acclimatize, and yesterday's rest was just what I needed to restore my energy.

The only bad thing is my sunburnt shoulders, but large quantities of aftersun lotion should take care of that. I think about the photos in the books in the bookshop and try to imagine myself on the mountain. Most of all, I fear the troubles we may have finding the right route. I remind myself that we must stay focused all the way and pay close attention to the infinite number of loose rocks. And again, the words 'it is going to be quite an experience' resound in my mind! I find my music player and scroll to Green

Day and one of my favorite songs, 'Good Riddance (Time of your life)':

So take the photographs and still frames in your mind.
Hang it on a shelf in good health and good time.
Tattoos of memories and dead skin on trial.
For what it's worth, it was worth all the while.
It's something unpredictable, but in the end it's right.
I hope you had the time of your life.

In the song, the approach to personal challenges does not quite comply with the kind of thoughts usually on my mind before a climb. Still, it works as a reminder to me that we should seek good experiences in life. On the Matterhorn, however, it is not about rushing things without thinking. It is first and foremost about creating a complete picture of the task and thereby achieving some kind of surplus mental capacity to anticipate the challenges ahead and make the right decisions. While thinking about how to best describe this feeling I am experiencing, a simple word pops up: excitement. Yes, that's it. I'm excited!

'Morning, Kjaer, coffee?'

'Thanks. What does the weather look like around the mountain?' The question shoots out when Brian, with a cup of coffee in his hand, pokes his head into the tent.

'Not a cloud...it's just perfect, so there is no excuse to stay in bed. Breakfast is served in five minutes.'

Brian has found a wooden board, which he has placed so that it rests on the back of two chairs. Combined with another two chairs, we have our own little theater: the lead role is played by Mrs.

Matterhorn, and we are the audience. Even though we are seated on the 'back row', looking through the binoculars makes us feel really close.

'Do you see anyone on the mountain?' I ask Brian, who is viewing the Hörnli Hut with breadcrumbs around his mouth.

'No, but I think I can see the Solvay Hut all the way up at 4003 meters,' he replies, while finishing his toast.

'Maybe someone is resting there? A lot of people would be able to make it to the emergency hut in four hours, so if they started at 4 am this morning, they should be there now.'

'I think we need a more powerful pair of binoculars to see such details, but I can definitely see that there is less snow than yesterday morning, so that's perfect. One more day with strong sun, and it would not be unrealistic to hope for a crampon-free climb.'

'Well, at least up to the shoulder above the Solvay Hut. From there, I don't think we can go on without them,' I answer.

I start laughing. Mostly within, though. We are such nerds! I am really happy with our enthusiasm. We are so busy checking out all sorts of details and expending masses of energy in order to prepare mentally. Usually, we share our thoughts, ideas and concerns, and indeed, at this moment there is a match: Brian is just as excited as I am, and he looks forward as much as I do to getting up there.

I sense that he is getting restless and wants to leave. It is past 9 am, and we agree to get ready for a 10 am departure from the campsite.

Despite the fact that it is Sunday, the town seems busy. At the railway station, the horses are neighing merrily as the stage coaches are being filled with tourists. Further up the street, shepherds are driving flocks of sheep which cause quite a commotion. In front of the shops, the owners are throwing dirt into the gutter, and the many electric cars are tooting their horns thus appearing to greet everyone. Nothing has changed in Zermatt.

At the tourist information office, we halt to check the latest weather forecast. It is just perfect. The next few days will be sunny with hardly any wind, no clouds and no precipitation. Fantastic! Together with sufficient acclimatization and the right climbing skills, the weather is the most important factor in a successful and safe climb. I smile and feel great that we have overcome the initial challenges. We stop at the bakery to buy some bread and cheese for lunch, which we plan to savor by the Hörnli Hut before exploring the lower section of the main climb.

Walking through the village, I continue my mental preparation. I try to frame our project in rational thoughts. It is not meditation or any kind of new-age voodoo. It just feels nice. I think about all the climbing projects Brian and I have completed together. It was only by coincidence that we met and began climbing together, but the fact that we are now approaching our biggest challenge together is by no means coincidental. When I am giving talks about mountaineering, people often ask me if I could imagine climbing with someone other than Brian. I could, but the friendship and security from a trusted and loyal climbing partner is just as important as the climbing itself. I know Brian's strengths and weaknesses, and he knows mine. For me, trust is most important.

There are hardly any people at the lift station. We discuss whether we should buy return tickets but agree to buy singles. If we end up coming down late from the mountain tomorrow night, the lift will be closed, and we are prepared to walk all the way to Zermatt if necessary. If we make it back earlier, we can probably buy a ticket from the upper station anyway.

The first lift takes us as far as Furi from where another lift brings us to the idyllic mountain lake Schwarzsee. The rest of the way up to the hut is on foot. Walking past Schwarzsee, for the first time I see the small chapel built many years ago as a token of gratitude to God. The legend describes a man who, for some time, had wandered helplessly around in thick clouds. As he got more and more scared, he prayed to God and promised to build a chapel if he could only get a clear view to get his bearings. The clouds spread and the sun shone down on the Schwarzsee. The man was satisfied. Now he knew his whereabouts and could continue his hike. He later returned to build the small chapel.

The hike from Schwarzsee at 2552 meters to the Hörnli Hut at 3260 meters takes a couple of hours according to the guide book. It is a relatively easy walk on good paths. I am annoyed by my shoulders, though; they seem to be on fire! I experiment with different settings of the carrying system of my backpack and end up carrying all the weight on my hips. Brian is carrying the rope and all the food, so my pack weighs only about 12 kilos. Since I know that the pack will be much lighter tomorrow morning, I am not concerned that it will inhibit my climbing.

We meet no other climbers on the way. We do meet, however, lots of tourists: many people use this section of the route for day trips. They have plenty of breaks to take photos or have refreshments, and when we pass them, they greet us and wish us luck. After about one hour, we approach the Hörnli Ridge where the track becomes steeper. It runs along the north face, and for the first time we feel a chilling wind. At the foot of the mountain, I can see the Matterhorn Glacier, separating our route on the Hörnli Ridge from the north western route on the Zmutt Ridge. Further northwest lies the massive Zmutt Glacier, behind which the characteristic summits of Dent Blanche and the Ober Gabelhorn rise.

While walking, I remember the guide book's introduction to climbing the Matterhorn. The book calls it 'one of the two or three most famous mountains in the world' and states that 'the Matterhorn will continue to remain an obligatory objective for a vast majority of alpinists.' Hopefully, they won't come away disappointed.

I put down my backpack on one of the benches which, together with the tables, create an almost café-like atmosphere outside the hut. Brian is already going through his pack to find the food. While I change my sweaty shirt with a dry one from my bag, I admire the mountain and the view. The enormous Furgg Glacier is impressive, to say the least. On the other hand, it is evident that it is only a pale shadow of what it used to be: the moraine debris clearly indicates the previous ice extent. Global warming will probably continue to provoke this shrinkage.

Every so often, rocks fall from the Matterhorn's infamous east wall to break the silence. They only stop when they reach the glacier far below. Holy shit, this is scary! I think. Better not be around when something like that happens. My thoughts are interrupted by another rockfall. Luckily, most falls seem to start on the east wall, a safe distance from our route on the Northeast Ridge.

A couple of tables away, a young guy is sitting with a giant pair of binoculars. He is busy looking at something on the mountain. Even if I strain my eyes, I cannot see what is keeping his attention. He does not mind letting me have a look, and I eagerly start searching for climbers on the route.

'I think I can see two people on the mountain,' I tell Brian and explain that they seem to be preparing an abseil from one of the numerous towers.

'Can I see?' he asks.

'Sure!' I hand him the binoculars and inform him that I saw a couple of climbers a hundred meters above the Grand Couloir.

'Hello boys!' somebody shouts. Peter and Phil have arrived.

'Hey, good to see you! How was your hike?'

Peter and Phil look tired, but the joy of reunion seems to renew their energy. As Phil gets his binoculars from his backpack, Peter tells us that the walk has taken them about four hours. He asks about our plans, and we inform him that after lunch we intend to climb the first bit of the route above the hut. They actually want to join us, but since they have decided to walk all the way back to Zermatt today, they decide to save time and energy. Instead, they will follow us through the binoculars.

The Irishmen are just as impressed as we are. It is overwhelming to sit here and look at the mountain, which seems to rise into the sky.

'No wonder it's called "The Majestic Summit",' I say.

As we talk, four men are coming down from the mountain. The two young guides look tired, but this is nothing compared to their clients – they look more dead than alive!

'Wow! If that's what you look like after the Matterhorn, we had better go to bed early, Kjaer!' Brian exclaims as he observes the arriving climbers.

'Have you seen them? They look like shit!' says Phil and shakes his head. He seems almost shocked.

One of the guides disappears into the hut and returns with two beers. They deserve it. Richard who runs the campsite told us that a lot of the guides live up here for several weeks at a time. Early in the morning, they set out to take clients to the top, and when they return, tired, in the afternoon, they have only a few hours to themselves before they meet up with a new client. Of course we are not supposed to feel pity for them; I am sure they consider themselves privileged to be able to make a living from their hobby. I actually feel sorrier for the clients that are hooked up with one guide during acclimatization just to be thrown into the arms of another only hours before they take on the challenge of their life.

In the climbing society, there are always plenty of rumors and stories going around. One is that the guides, who get paid the same whether they succeed in getting clients all the way to the summit or not, climb at a forced pace to exhaust clients in order to make them give up and turn back after a few hours. In this way, the guides can return to the hut much sooner and have time to relax before the next client arrives. Not very sympathetic and probably not very true! Naturally the guides are interested in climbing as fast as possible in order to reduce the time spent on the mountain. They are also interested, however, in achieving impressive statistics and a good reputation.

The majority of the tourists have already left to make it down in time to get the last lift back to Zermatt. Peter and Phil are getting ready to follow them. They invite us to meet them at The Brown Cow tomorrow night. We accept, of course, and express our gratitude that they take such an interest in our endeavors.

They say goodbye and wish us luck. To my distress, the farewell escalates somewhat: Phil holds my hand a bit longer than what seems natural, and his eyes say something I don't understand. He tells me to take care up there, takes his pack and leaves.

When they are out of sight, I tell Brian that I think the Irishmen worry more about us than they let on. I try to explain what I saw in Phil's eyes.

'I think he's scared, Brian.'

'Yeah, maybe. Let's take that as yet another reminder to be careful,' he answers.

'How are you?' I ask.

'I feel a bit overwhelmed by being here, but other than that I'm perfectly fine. How about you?'

'I can't stop thinking about what I saw in his eyes. I have never experienced anything like that before.'

'I can see how it must seem a bit odd, but I didn't notice it. Are you all right?'

'Yes. Just let me inform the guardian that we have arrived, and then we are ready to take a closer look at the mountain.'

'Splendid! I'll find the small binoculars...anything else to take?'

'The guide book perhaps?'

'Sure!'

A few meters above the hut we find the tent site – the only alternative to the hut. On the small plateau lies a man. He is sleeping outside his tent. Just next to his tent, there is a big sign saying that tenting is prohibited. The big rocks scattered around the tent give a clear indication of why: the spot is extremely exposed to rock falls. It does not take us long to agree that we have made the right decision choosing the hut. Once past the plateau, we traverse a small snow field leading to a small but steep rock wall. The track in the snow is deep, and it feels safe to walk here. On the other hand, I cannot help noticing that a fall to the right will not end until the Matterhorn Glacier a couple of hundred meters below. This passage will require some concentration. At the steep rock wall, we are welcomed by a memorial plaque mounted right at the start of the climb. The plaque tells the sad story of a climber. I get the chills but continue up the wall using the fixed ropes. I know the story; I know that people die on the Matterhorn every year. I also know that nothing is gained by being affected by these constant reminders. Like so many times before, I tell myself not to think about what can go wrong but rather to focus on what to do to prevent anything from going wrong. Brian has also seen the plaque, but as he does not comment on it, neither do I.

From the top of the wall, we continue through a labyrinth of tracks along the ridge. If it had not been for a thick layer of loose gravel, this would have made a fine walk. Again and again, I slide on the soft surface and curse the difficult conditions. I use so much energy trying not to slip; in several places, the track is sloping to such an extent that a slide would almost certainly become a long fall, a fall I probably would not survive.

'It stinks walking on this shit!' I complain to Brian.

'I know. I have the feeling that this isn't the most obvious track, but when I look around, the other tracks look just as hopeless.'

'You're right. Hey – look over there! There are people coming down,' I say while pointing to a track further up on the ridge.

'Right, let's aim for their position.'

We continue in this manner, constantly searching for a better and more secure track. The next group we meet have chosen a path below us. Eventually, I realize that no track is better than another. The secret may be to stick to the same track and focus on walking safely.

A minor rockfall further up breaks the silence. It sounds as if it comes from what is known as the first couloir. I suggest to Brian that we end our exploration when we reach it. There is no need to expose ourselves to any unnecessary risks. Still, it is valuable to identify the best track so that we do not have to struggle with that in the dark tomorrow morning. We agree to continue up along the edge of the couloir and from there try to spot the best place to cross it.

At a safe distance, we try to point out a good spot for crossing. It does not seem too bad. We have to be fast, though. The couloirs of the Matterhorn are dreaded amongst climbers: big piles of rocks are falling down every day, and many climbers have taken their last steps here.

On the other hand, we get excited at the sight of the towers on the other side of the couloir. Many of them seem to offer nice, sustained climbing. But which ones are parts of the route? We search through the guide book but find no answer. If we choose the wrong ones, we may waste valuable time, and we may be forced to abseil down again.

Next to us are two climbers, who are also exploring the Matterhorn. They are Andrea and Rich from Wales. They tell us that they have trained for a year for this project, and that they are extremely excited about finally being here. They also ask enthusiastically about our plans. For more than one hour, we sit on the rocks, trying to figure out, bit by bit, which track to follow and which towers to climb. Andrea talks about their acclimatization efforts which, contrary to ours, ended in a big mess, primarily because they could not find the hut they aimed for and so had to continue to another one, which, as it turned out, had no vacant beds. Being forced to travel to a third hut, they had to give up their climbing plans. While Andrea talks, we witness another enormous rockfall.

On the way back to the hut, I notice the ease with which the Welshmen are climbing despite them being around 40 years old. The steep sections do not cause them any problems. Their excellent technique and their positive attitude will help them to make it to the summit. The unknown factor is of course their acclimatization; if that is in place, I believe they are going to make it.

Brian and I have been taken to our dormitory. In the small room full of bunks, we have emptied out our backpacks and are now trying to cut back even further on their contents for the climb. Each person sleeping in the hut gets a plastic box to store things in while away on the mountain. Of course we will be using our mountain boots, gaiters, jackets, pants, fleece, hats and gloves. We will also need our helmets, head torches, harnesses, belay device, crampons, axe and rope. Our shared equipment is scattered on the bed and we try to decide what to bring and what to leave behind. What will we be needing? We choose some slings, carabiners, camming devices, ice screws, a snow anchor and some quickdraws. The rest goes into the plastic box. I check the first aid gear again. Together with the camera and 2.5 liters of water, it goes into the backpack. Brian packs the guide book, map and compass, as well as an extra pair of gloves. We are ready!

In front of the Hörnli Hut, a group of climbers enjoy the evening sun. Soon, the last rays will disappear behind the Matterhorn, and it will be too cold to sit outside in T-shirts. One team is repairing their equipment, while another is sorting theirs the same way as we have just done. At the reception desk, Andrea is looking through the postcards. She is especially interested in one of the summit shots that shows the cross on the so-called Italian summit. It is actually a mistake to call the summit of the Matterhorn a Swiss summit. Just as it is wrong to call the 1.5 meter lower "top" the Italian summit. As a matter of fact, the border runs precisely through both summits. Those who experience standing on the summit of the Matterhorn may therefore be standing with one leg in Switzerland and the other in Italy. Andrea really likes the postcard and states that she will send herself one when she returns from the summit. She also tells us that she, for more than a year, has had a poster of the Matterhorn glued to the back of her toilet door in Wales. I smile at her but can tell she is serious. Climbing the Matterhorn is so much more than just another day in the mountains. To her, it is a dream close to coming true!

The atmosphere in the large dining hall is relaxed. Climbers hang around in small groups, talking, and the hut staff prepare to serve the three course dinner. We take a seat with our new friends and ask them about life in Wales. Rich tells us how they both quit good jobs and left their family and friends behind in London. Instead, they have bought a small house in Wales and lined up with the other unemployed. He explains that they sought a life without stress and with more time to spend on climbing and being in the wild. Andrea cuts in with anecdotes from their climbing adventures and keeps repeating that we must come to visit them.

We spend another hour in their company, and naturally the conversation turns towards the Matterhorn and the expectations we each have. Like us, they have prepared everything in order to be among the first teams to leave the hut. We all know that each team has to manage on their own, but, still, it is a popular strategy to follow the guided teams on the lower sections where the mess of false tracks is likely to make it difficult to find the right route. On the other hand, we know that it is an almost impossible task: the guides will start out at a high pace, and we are bound to lose them on the first steep passages.

I look around trying to estimate how many climbers we will be on the mountain tomorrow. At dinner, we were about 30 people, but among them several could be hikers that use the hut as a stop-over for an extended hike. As far as I can tell, there are only five or six guides in the hut, so my guess is that there will only be about 20 people on the mountain. This is good news. The more climbers, the higher the risk that someone will start a rockfall and the longer the queues will be at the difficult points. On the way down, however, there may be more people, as it is common for climbers coming from the Italian side to use the Hörnli Hut when they come down the mountain.

'It's so big!' I say to Brian later as we stand outside the front door staring at the mountain in the fading light.

'I know.' I begin to realize what Allan and Soren meant when they said that you climb and climb forever without getting any closer to the summit.

'What do you think when you look at it?' I ask Brian.

'I think about what it'll be like to stand on the summit.'

'It's gonna be awesome...but we have to keep moving at a steady pace if we're to succeed. We can't allow ourselves too many breaks.'

'You're right, and we'll just do what we always do: the one who feels strong at a given time is in front.'

'Sure!'

'What do you think?' asks Brian.

'First and foremost, I look forward to having passed the first couloir…the approach is a bit of a nightmare with all that loose gravel and the sloping tracks.'

'At least we know what's coming…'

'Have you noticed the temperature? I don't think we are below zero.'

We are interrupted by a crashing rockfall. Maybe it was just a small pebble that started it. It gets to me every time I hear one of these rockfalls. The frequent falls remind us that we must never lose concentration. The route will be full of loose rocks that we must spot and avoid. Otherwise, our expedition may easily end up in an accident. Many climbers have ended their climb on the Matterhorn because they fell on the loose rocks or were hit by flying rocks, kicked loose above them.

I often think that I fully understand why non-climbers wonder what makes climbers expose themselves to such dangers. It may seem paradoxical that we, in order to increase safety, spend so much time investigating and exploring only to learn about deaths and accidents and discover new potential dangers. I am convinced, though, that our research efforts help reduce the risks dramatically – that our knowledge, skills and thorough preparations make our climbing much safer.

It is 9.30 pm and soon the lights will be turned off. Many have already gone to bed. At the tables, a few experienced climbers are still discussing routes and exchanging experiences. Two men are uncoiling their rope and adjusting their gaiters, while a third is sharpening his axe. Behind the guide's regular table, I discover a number of photos which, together with memorial plaques, honor the guides who have lost their lives on the mountain. Many have probably died because clients have lost their balance and pulled them down. There are also newspaper clippings about climbing in the old days. All together, this tells the story of the majestic, fascinating and frightening Matterhorn.

President Roosevelt on the Matterhorn

On August 4th, 1881, Theodore Roosevelt (1858-1919), who later became the American President (1901-1909), climbed the Matterhorn, guided by Mathias Zumtaugwald. During the honeymoon with his first wife, Roosevelt found the time to climb several mountains around Zermatt, including the Matterhorn, a climb he describes in the letter to his sister Anna (Bysie). It was only 16 years after the first successful scent. Even though fixed ropes had been put up at certain passages on the route, it was – and still is – a strenuous and risky task to climb the Matterhorn.

Darling Bysie, Zermatt, August 5, 1881

Day before yesterday, at nine in the morning, I started off, accompanied by two guides, to make the ascent of the Matterhorn. I was anxious to go up it because it is reputed very difficult, and a man who has been up it can fairly claim to have taken his degree as, at any rate, a subordinate kind of mountaineer.

At 6 o'clock in the evening we reached the small hut, half a cavern, where we spent the night; it was on the face of a cliff, up which we climbed by a rope forty feet long, and the floor was covered with ice a foot deep. The mountain is so steep that snow will not remain on the crumbling, jagged rocks, and possesses a certain somber interest from the number of people that have lost their lives on it. Accidents, however, are generally due to either rashness, or else to a combination of timidity and fatigue; a fairly hardy man, cautious but not cowardly, with good guides, has little to fear. Still, there is enough peril to make it exciting, and the work is very laborious, being as much with the hands as the feet, and (very unlike the Jungfrau) as hard coming down as going up.

We left the hut at three-forty and, after seeing a most glorious sunrise which crowned the countless snow peaks and billowy, white clouds with a strange crimson iridescence, reached the summit at seven, and were down at the foot of the Matterhorn proper by one. It was like going up and down enormous stairs on your hands and knees for nine hours. We then literally ran down the foothills to Zermatt, reaching it at half past three.

It had been excessively laborious, and during the journey I was nearer giving up than on the Jungfrau, but I was not nearly so tired afterwards, and in fact felt as fresh as ever after a cup of tea and a warm bath; went to table d'hote as usual and afterwards over to see the Gardiners, and coming back we spent the rest of the evening with Mrs. Baylies, Miss Cornelia & Edmund.

Your Loving Brother

The Matterhorn for Life

On the Internet, a long list of personal accounts of experiences on the Matterhorn can be found. One of the authors is Nyle K. Walton from the USA:

> I would like to add some facts about my ascent of the Matterhorn accomplished when I was 48.
>
> After returning to my army post in Rochefort from Zermatt, I read in the Stars and Stripes a news article about a young American from Denver and his English companion who fell to their deaths from the Matterhorn during a guideless climb. Four years later I returned to Zermatt and found their gravestones in the village cemetery at the end of a row of other victims of alpine tragedies.
>
> I will forever be grateful to Emil Julen, probably in his seventies by now if he is still alive. He was my competent guide who got this novice to the top and back. His fee was only forty dollars. There was much

less demand for guides back then.

I still have a Kodachrome photograph enlarged to poster size of me standing across the valley from the rearing "Lion of the Alps," framed between two pine trees. It was taken on August 4, a day after the climb. I was seventy pounds lighter then and far more fit than I am today. In ten days, I will turn seventy.

Ah, youth! Why must it be wasted on the young?

September 30th, 2001

The Matterhorn

Monday, July 7th

'This is it, Kjaer, are you awake?' asks Brian.

'Err...I think so,' I manage to answer while I try to figure out where I am and what is going on around me.

'Someone just knocked on the door. It's 3.30 am and it's time to go.'

'OK!'

I have slept really badly. First, I could not fall asleep, and when I finally did, two men came in and rattled around in the dark. One of them chose the bed next to me where he kept moving around forever. There I was again – unable to fall asleep. Right now I feel like I haven't slept at all.

'Hey, are you awake, Kjaer? We need to go, man!'

'Damn! Sorry! Give me two minutes.'

If I was not wide awake before, I certainly am now. I find it quite embarrassing that Brian has had to call twice.

I get dressed as fast as possible. Over my long underwear, I wear my heavy duty mountain pants that have proved their worth on previous trips. The material is windproof, and the long zippers on the sides enable me to cool off easily when in the sun. I am almost ready; I just need to lace my boots. I struggle a bit with my socks.

They must fit the foot properly: even the smallest fold may cause blisters. That's it. I'm ready.

We rush down to the dinning hall and join the other climbers.

'Would you like a cup of tea?' asks Brian

'Err...yes please,' I reply while I try to spot some coffee – without success.

'You had better get some food down, you,' laughs Brian, who sounds like my grandmother trying to persuade me to eat too much of everything.

I can tell that he also sees the parallel and laughs while he lectures me about the importance of energy intake and assures me that the tea we drink now will do us good later. Oh yeah...Brian is certainly awake.

Andrea and Rich are at the table next to us. They are already tied into their rope. Besides a friendly 'good morning', they have not said much. They seem really focused. I cannot help thinking about Andrea's story about the poster on the Welsh toilet door. I really hope they make it.

Suddenly, all hell breaks loose. Some of the guides get up and put on their harnesses, and it seems like everybody else takes that as a signal to do the same. What was a tense silence a few minutes ago, is now an inferno of instructions in different languages and people running back and forth. Everybody tries to squeeze down an extra piece of bread while tightening their harness and putting on their head torch. Whereas most people choose to do it indoors in the light, a few people are fumbling around outside in the dark.

I take one end of our rope and hand the other to Brian, who is adjusting the shoulder pads on his backpack. We only need to tie in and we can set off. That's it!

'Are you ready, Brian?' I ask as we stand outside the hut trying to get used to the dark.

'Sure, let's go! Do you see any guides?'

'No, but I think they are only about 50 meters in front of us. Come on, we'll catch them before the snowfield.'

'I can't believe that it isn't any colder. It's 4.15 am, and it's definitely above zero. I'm really surprised!' says Brian as we chase the guides.

The strategy is to maintain a good pace at the beginning in order to keep up with the climbers who know the route. We know, however, that it is only a question of time before the groups will spread and we will be left to find the route on our own.

The first bit up to the small plateau is soon over. From here, we cross the snowfield to get to the small steep rock wall with the memorial plaque. Crossing the snowfield, I remember an accident I had on the Kebnekaise Glacier in Sweden in 1999. Like now, we had to cross a sloping snowfield, but the snow collapsed under my feet, and I fell down the steep mountain side. Luckily, I managed to stop my fall at the last minute, but the experience was an everlasting lesso n.

I carefully step out onto the snow. On my right, there is a significant drop to the Matterhorn Glacier, and I have no difficulty imagining that a fall here would leave me seriously injured – at best. I concentrate on every movement: first the right food and then the left. After every step, I wait a moment before taking the next one to make sure I am in balance. One more step and another one. From here, the gradient eases, and the last meters to the rock wall are easy.

Everything is dark around us. Still, I recognize Andrea in her characteristic down jacket in the small crowd below the wall. One by one, climbers are pulling themselves up by the fixed ropes, and they disappear behind a smaller wall above. Then it is Andrea and Rich; they climb the wall as elegantly and easily as I saw them climb yesterday.

'Good luck!' I yell to them as we wait for our turn on the fixed ropes.

'Thanks...you too...we'll see you on the summit!' Rich shouts back.

'Yeah, take care guys!' Andrea contributes before disappearing.

It seems that this place is the gateway to the Matterhorn. This is the door we all have to go through to be let into the climb.

By the aid of the fixed ropes, we are soon on the small plateau above. From here, we have about twenty minutes of walking slightly uphill before we reach the first of three couloirs. Amongst numerous rock formations and countless towers, the big couloirs are among the most identifiable features. Unfortunately, these giant chutes are also renowned for their treacherous rockfalls. The majority of the rockfalls we heard yesterday surely came from these. This is exactly why the guides, a couple of years ago, decided to change the route and cross the second couloir higher up on the mountain.

After only five minutes on the sloping gravel tracks, we are lost, or, at least, we are not walking on the track we decided to follow yesterday. Ahead of us, we can see a small line of lights: the front groups, which are probably the guided teams, are closing in on the first couloir. Despite the weather being mild and clear, we benefit from our head torches. It is still dark, and our beams of light enable us to see 15-20 meters ahead.

As we walk, I decide that from now on I will focus on climbing only. There is the Matterhorn and nothing else. During the last week, my head has been filled with questions of all sorts, but primarily practical questions related to the climb. Together, we have spent a lot of time thinking about and discussing the strategy for climbing this mountain. Now we must trust the plan. We must focus.

'OK Steffen, we've got to cross quickly; I think we may even have to run but...we don't have enough rope out to run one at a time...don't you think this is where we are supposed to cross?' asks Brian when we reach the first couloir.

'Yes, but we have to be really careful...and fast,' I answer.

'You first?' suggests Brian.

'OK, but be prepared to follow me...I will try to run across.'

The couloir is about ten meters wide, maybe 15. It is hard to tell exactly. Halfway across, we have to descend slightly to reach a corner around which the route continues.

'Right, this is it,' I say as I take a last look at my faithful climbing partner, who seems just as focused as I am.

'OK, I'm ready,' he answers.

The couloir is like a wide moraine field set at a challenging gradient. Despite it being dark, my head torch provides enough light for me to see ahead as I run. Behind me, I can hear Brian, and I know he is now on the same obstacles I have just passed. Above us, an enormous wall rises, waiting to drop loose rocks.

Almost there! With each step I take, rocks roll away under my feet. Focus! C'mon, Steffen, move it! Two meters, then one meter, then quickly around the corner. I grab the rope and pull as fast as I can to prevent Brian from tripping over it.

'Right, Brian, what do we do from here?' I ask as I try to recall the images from yesterday's exploration.

It looks as if we have two options. We can either climb a steep channel above us or continue to the left along the track following the wall. I am a bit annoyed that we are struggling with the route already, but I also know that this will probably be the rule rather than the exception today. This is only a teaser for what awaits us on the rest of the mountain. Above us, I can see numerous scratch marks from other climbers' crampons, but the same goes for the track going left.

'I don't know, but we must move on...let's go left,' Brian suggests and points to the many marks from past climbers having made the same decision.

I move on and look around. Not a soul. So much for that plan – we had hoped to follow the guides on this section, but they are long gone.

The track ends here. To the left it drops all the way to the enormous Furgg Glacier. Either we go back and climb the steep wall we left ten minutes ago, or we try this wall, which looks just as steep.

I look at Brian.

'Can you climb that?' he asks.

'I don't know, but let's try. I just need your cams and nuts,' I answer as I prepare myself.

Brian hands me his part of the rack and prepares to belay me.

I look up and let the light sweep over the wall. The route seems obvious but also difficult. Plenty of crampon marks to follow.

I would probably have benefited from wearing crampons, I think, as I try to balance my big mountain boots on the small ledges. Above me to the right, I can see a crack where I can place some protection. I move carefully; the darkness, the boots, the cold rock and the weight on my shoulders from my backpack contribute to make this pitch more exciting than I prefer it to be. I place a cam in the crack and move on. I focus and try to hold on to small holds while searching for bigger ones; I genuinely look forward to the end of this fumbling in the dark. My left foot slips. There are no alternatives. The foot slips again. Below me, I can barely see the dimly lit cam. Has it moved? To put it bluntly: the situation sucks. I am running out of strength, and in my current position, I cannot move without losing my balance.

'Uuuhh...Jorgensen, I don't know...I'm not sure I can do it. Do you feel like giving it a go?' I ask while fighting the backpack, which is now more on my side than on my back.

'Sure, but do you think I can?'

'I don't know, but I am coming down. Just let me place some gear for you to lower me.'

Shit! I really hate the fact that I have to give up. It is absolutely fine if Brian can do it, but we are wasting a lot of time, and we are not getting closer to the summit.

Brian prepares for his attempt. I consider offering to take his pack but end up not saying anything. I will wait and see how he manages. Of course, climbing will be easier without the extra kilos constantly challenging your balance, but this is a long climb, and we cannot afford to lose anything. Our equipment is already limited to an absolute minimum, and the consequences of losing a backpack speaks for itself: goodbye axe, crampons, clothes, food and water. The risk is just too big.

Brian is doing well. The first part, below the protection I placed, goes fine. But now he has reached the point from where I had to return. Besides his heavy breathing, indicating that he is working hard, no sound can be heard from him. So I keep quiet as well. Come on, Brian. Come on! Suddenly, high above me, I can see that he is moving, and the rope is pulled up at a steady pace. Yes! In a moment, he will shout to me that he is safe.

'Wow, this is beautiful...no, it's extremely beautiful – have you seen it, Jorgensen?' I ask and point towards the summit.

'Well, yes! – I have been here for quite a while now,' replies Brian with a big smile.

The transition from the troublesome wall to this amazing view is like coming to a different world.

'But have you seen the light, Jorgensen...it's so amazing!'

This experience takes first place. I have never seen anything like it. Above us, the Matterhorn is glowing in the most beautiful red colors imaginable. Not a single cloud. Only the sun, painting its morning colors on the most gorgeous mountain in the world.

While Brian reads out loud from the guide book, I try to identify the big couloirs mentioned in the book as well as figure out which way to choose around the gendarmes. Some of them are huge; they rise up high into the air and serve as landmarks. From where we stand, though, it is impossible to decide which are the ones mentioned in the book.

In front of us, crampon marks lead everywhere. Which ones should we follow?

In the confusing mess of marks, we choose the direction by means of intuition. We have not even been on the mountain for two hours, and we have already wasted half an hour on blind alleys and difficult passages. We are both aware that our chance of summiting will disappear into thin air – literally – if we do not manage to find a rhythm and start taking in the 1100 meters of altitude still in front of us. I realize that my concerns have not been underestimated. This mountain will only be climbed by those who manage to combine will power with determination and to maintain control; by those who manage to control frustration and by those who manage to focus on the summit while they analyze every step and hold on the way.

It is not the technical side of affairs that is causing problems. The level of difficulty matches the information we have acquired. But still, my body and brain are on high alert. Every movement must be coordinated to make sure that I do not start a rock slide, or worse, a rockfall. Before I grab onto something or place my foot, I determine if it is safe or not. Normally, the lead climber will choose the route, but on this mountain, any wrong decision threatens to lead us far astray. Hence, I constantly confer with Brian about which way to go. From time to time, we stop for a few seconds while Brian reads out loud from the guide book, and, just as often, we are forced to climb back down or change course. I have now accepted that this is how it will be the rest of the way. Doing so has brought me past frustration and replaced it with a determination that almost seems new to me. I actually don't think that the people I know back home – my family, friends and colleagues - would recognize this side of me. To be honest, I don't think I would be able to mobilize determination of these dimensions in day-to-day life at home. But this is different. Under these conditions, there is room for nothing else than Brian, myself and our common goal: to reach the summit of this beautiful mountain and return safely.

'Gee...wow...this is insane!' shouts Brian.

At a safe distance from us on the infamous east wall, a giant rockfall is thundering down the mountain and crushes everything on its way. It started several hundred meters above us, and, like an avalanche, it picks up speed and grows in mass the further it travels. Now and then, it looks as if it is going to stop, but just as we think it has died out, a boulder bangs into another one and the show goes on. It does not take a lot of imagination to figure out what would happen if we or other climbers got caught below a rockfall like that.

‘It’s unreal...I’m not sure I understand how this mountain, day by day, year after year, drops so much rock and still stands,’ I say to Brian.

‘I know. It’s unbelievable...but what do we do now?’

‘Good question. Do you think we have come too far away from the ridge?’ I ask.

‘There are plenty of small tracks...but many seem to stop here. I don’t know...maybe we should try to climb that chute over there,’ suggests Brian and points to a corner several meters above us.

‘Let’s...I actually think I can see some slings right at the top of it.’

Another dead end! From here, all we can do is abseil back down. At least, the view is nice. For the first time, I can see the Solvay Hut, which we know is placed at 4003 meters, and for the first time, we can see the next several hundred meters of climbing and not just the next twenty or so.

The distance between us is short. We decided long ago not to climb in traditional style with the first placing protection while being belayed by the second – it would be way too time consuming. As a result, I don’t have the time to inform Brian that this route is another dead end before he starts climbing:

‘It’s a dead end!’ I shout down to him.

‘OK, do you want me to stay here?’ he asks, halfway up the corner.

‘No, I think you should come up here. I can see all the way to the Hut..., and I think it would be worthwhile to spend a minute or two trying to figure out the route from here.’

I place the rope behind a small rock tower and belay Brian the last few meters. Normally, I would take the opportunity to throw in a teasing comment, even if there is nothing to tease him about. However, here – now – I don't even think of it. Instead, I gaze at the summit still so far away. But we are getting closer. Everywhere I can see slings swaying silently in the light breeze: red, yellow, blue, black, white, new and old. Loads of slings! Suddenly, it dawns upon me that they are not showing us the right way, but, rather, 'this is where our track ended, don't bother.'

After another read through the guide book's recommendations, we prepare to abseil. The climbing up to this view point was not hard, but it seems unwise to climb down. While Brian is untying himself, I check the tape sling we are going to use for an anchor. It looks strong; it is neither old nor worn, and the rock spike it is placed around is not going anywhere. I pull half the rope through the sling, tie the rope ends together and throw the coil down to the bottom of the corner.

That's it! Brian quickly moves to the side, and I pull down the rope. Let's go! I look around to see if we can climb the next bit without the rope, but no. The area is a labyrinth of differently sized boulders and towers we have to climb around and over. It would be too dangerous, and we will surely need the rope in a matter of minutes.

'Holy smoke! What's going on?' asks Brian in a voice that does not seem like a question but rather a statement that something is very wrong.

Instead of answering, I just stare in the same direction.

'Yes; what is going on?' I finally stutter, while I stare at a guide and his client.

'He is completely exhausted,' Brian exclaims.

'Certainly seems like a good decision to get him off the mountain…, but it looks like it might be difficult,' I answer. 'He can barely stand on his feet.'

The client is tottering around. His lights are out; the empty gaze in his eyes indicates that he has surrendered and put his life into the hands of his guide. Right now, the guide is the difference between life and death for this climber. I recognize the guide as one of the young guides we saw at the Hörnli Hut yesterday. He is strong. Still, it is a constant fight to keep them both on the track. The guide holds his client on a short rope, but the man is still all over the place; stumbling and swaying. His bodily movements are without any coordination whatsoever. Every so often, he begins to fall, head first, but every time, he is saved by the rope and the strong guide.

'Do you think he is suffering from altitude sickness?' asks Brian.

'I am sure of it…, but no, no…look at that,' I say, frightened.

The downward slope is steep, and the guide fights with all he has got. The client attempt to sit down, which is actually not possible as there is nothing to sit on. Instead, he is held back by the guide, who commands him back on his feet. I consider how we may be of help but quickly realize that there is not much we can do. The guide is all too aware of the condition of his client. He has made the right decision, and the only thing to do is to get down swiftly.

This may be an inbuilt risk of the new system. In 2003, the guides decided that clients had to document some level of experience, and if they could not, they had to practice with a guide before attempting the Matterhorn. This decision is sound and wise. However, due to the distance between Zermatt and the Hörnli Hut, it is often the case that a client practices with one guide and is sent to meet another guide at the Hörnli Hut. This new guide does not know the client well, and he may therefore be less able to read the signs of fatigue or reaction to altitude.

As we are tying ourselves into the rope again, they pass right by us – the young guide and his client. They stop. The client is still in front, but despite the fact that the ground is more level here and relatively easy to walk on, nothing happens. The man has an apathetic expression on his face, and without any sign of initiative in his empty eyes, he just stands there. Then he closes his eyes and sways a little back and forth. He is asleep, standing!

'Move on…we gotta get down!' the guide yells to his client.

It is not that the man does not want to cooperate. But he is completely gone and unable to take care of himself. The guide knows it; he passes the client, pulls at the rope and so pulls the man out of dreamland. This is how they continue; one step at a time, then the guide pulls the rope, then another step.

At this moment, it is completely clear to me that this cannot be the point: climbing the Matterhorn is, for many mountaineers, the biggest goal, a dream. Goals are something you qualify and work for, determined to achieve. This client is not qualified. I am sure he has the dream, but he should not be here. Under different conditions, he may be qualified; maybe he is poorly acclimatized and therefore struck by altitude sickness. I will never know, but in this state, he is putting himself, his guide and the rest of us on the mountain in danger.

'Let's go...are you ready, Brian?'

'Sure, let's move,' answers Brian.

We continue up the steep section on which, a few minutes ago, we watched the client tottering at the end of the rope.

I move quickly and focused. Looking at the summit makes me repeat silently what I already know: there is a long, long way to go. Even if climbing the corner gave us an overview of the route, it has cost us a lot of precious time.

The route on the rock takes us further towards the ridge. It seems right. Soon we are climbing on the ridge proper. From here, on our right, I can see a major part of the Matterhorn's terrifying and infamous north face. Further down, I can see the broken Matterhorn Glacier, and, on the horizon, I see all the mountains I was watching on the way up yesterday. We are still below the more difficult passages, but, at the same time, so high up that it would take considerable time to get down should something unfortunate happen.

The rock in front of me is polished by the steps of time. Crampons have left a yellowish color on the rock, and in that way the marks of the past act as a guide. If it is the right way though. Again I am in doubt. For every step I take, the track narrows and becomes less clear.

'Well, I'm afraid this was another blank,' I say, laughing, as I realize the track ends below a steep rock wall.

'Hmm...can we climb it?' asks Brian.

'We may be able to, but we have no idea where we will end up...maybe it will lead us to an isolated plateau – like the corner we climbed earlier.'

'You're right, but what to do then?' questions Brian.

'I think we have to backtrack and try to go a bit further out on the east wall. The route may be on the other side of this tower,' I suggest.

'OK!'

As we backtrack, I think about the paradox that the mountain seems so perfect when watched from a distance, but appears completely different when you are so close. Some have called it 'ugly,' but to me it is merely a giant labyrinth in which the "right" route does not seem to exist.

'This may be it, then,' says Brian as he points to a track, which first takes a sharp right turn and then leads through some enormous boulders.

'Maybe...let's try it. We can always backtrack again,' I laugh.

It is like a revelation. From here we can see the Solvay Hut again, and I get the clear impression that we can reach it in an hour or maybe less - well, at least if we manage to stay on track. I can see a big gendarme on the ridge below the hut, and for the first time, we have a clear, unambiguous point of orientation. There are several pieces of fixed equipment here – wires and iron stakes. Some of them seem reliable whereas others have long passed their sell-by date. But most important, they indicate that we are still on track. Step by step, movement by movement, we are getting closer to the hut. Even if the summit is our main goal, we focus on the hut. This is our refuge and a most welcome spot for our first real break.

'Hey Steffen, look out there!' Brian yells somewhere behind me. He points to the left towards the many boulders of the east wall.

'Shit! It's Andrea and Rich'.

'They are going down!'

'Do you think they have given up? They cannot have made it all the way to the summit already, can they?'

I am a bit stirred by this; they seemed so strong. Perhaps their acclimatization was not sufficient after all. I feel pity for them; I remember Andrea with the postcards in the hut. This was her dream, their dream.

'Andrea! Rich! Are you going down?'

'Yeah, we couldn't make it. We are too tired already!' answers Rich.

'Oh, I'm sorry!' I shout back.

'Thanks! But you guys...you'll make it. We know that!'

'Thanks! Take care...and Andrea, leave your address at the hut, and I'll send you a postcard!' I shout, but I am not sure they hear m e.

The distance between us makes it impossible to have more of a conversation. I worry about them being so far out on the east wall; as a matter of fact, they are terrifyingly close to where we saw the enormous rockfall an hour ago. There is nothing we can do, though. They are too far away. We must push on.

This section of the route is not that steep. The challenge is more or less to stay on-route and keep our balance as we scramble over boulders and rocks. In some places, we can walk in an upright position, in other places, the route demands a firm grip on a rock. I focus on every move and evaluate every hold in order to avoid relying on something loose. And I have this voice in my head constantly reminding me to look up to avoid leading us off-route. It's the same voice that, after every move, says: move on, Steffen! I am far from convinced that we will succeed in reaching the summit; the unknowns are too numerous. But I know that we stand a good chance if we continue this way.

Now I can see the Moseley Slab.

The Moseley Slab is named after the American William Moseley, who, on August 14th, 1879, died on this passage. It is not at all impassable, but it is steep, and the tragic story reminds us to be careful. The death of William Moseley was in many ways a turning point in the history of the Matterhorn. There had been no serious accidents on the Matterhorn since the tragedy that hit Whymper's team after the first ascent in 1865. 14 years on, people may have come to think of the Matterhorn as an easy mountain. Perhaps this was why a nonchalant William Moseley refused to be part of his team and decided to climb what we now know as the Moseley Slab without a rope and wearing leather boots which, with nails in their soles, did not help him much on this steep wall. Halfway up, he fell. Moseley's accident thus became another chapter in the dramatic history of the Matterhorn and, to the rest of us, a reminder that success on the mountain depends entirely on our ability to objectively evaluate the dangers and make wise decisions on the way.

'OK, Brian, this is Moseley Slab!'

'Yeah...do you want to lead?'

'No problem,' I say and start right away.

At first sight, the rock looks firmer than the lower sections. As I climb, however, I realize that it is just as loose as the rest. On my right, the wall is vertical and on my left it is loose and, in some places, overhanging! I decide to climb in the middle so there are fairly good holds on both sides of me.

We are still using running belays, and although I have the opportunity to ask Brian to stay at the foot of the slab until I reach the top, I give him the signal to follow me right away. This saves us a lot of time. Even if the climbing is not that hard, the wall is quite steep. I take the time to place some protection. Every time I do so, I ask Brian to stay still for a while in order to keep the rope tight between us. Just as I have to stop whenever he is removing the gear I have put in. In this manner, we climb the 30 meters to the top of the Moseley Slab quite efficiently. Next stop: the Solvay Hut.

At 4003 meters, the Solvay Hut serves as an emergency shelter, a point of orientation and a lunch spot for most of the climbers. It should not go unnoticed that the hut is an impressive building, erected by skilful and brave craftsmen on one of the most spectacular building sites in the world.

The original hut was built during World War I as a means of preventing some of the many accidents on the Matterhorn. The story tells us that the building materials were transported by mules from Schwarzsee to the Hörnli Hut, and the rest of the way with the use of a provisional lift system. The hut, then bigger than the current version, was financed by the Belgian businessman Ernest Solvay and inaugurated in 1917. Since then, it has been repaired many times, and today it is equipped with an emergency radio, mattresses and blankets.

'So this is where the Italian guide fell to his death when Soren and Allan were up here,' states Brian, while looking up as if he wants to check that we are not going to be hit by falling climbers.

It is 9.15 am. We sit in front of the Solvay Hut on the narrow concrete platform. It is our first break since we left the hut five hours ago, and we realize that we are one hour behind the guide book time for this part of the climb. That is not too bad considering the hour or so we have spent searching for the right way. We try to relax a little but agree to keep the break short. We just need something to eat and drink, then we must move on.

'He just flew by them when he fell...imagine sitting here and witnessing that,' I mumble into the air.

'Do you remember the exact story?' asks Brian.

I do. Actually, I remember it well. As part of the preparation for our expedition, I have read Soren Pedersen's article describing the accident several times. I also had a long chat with him on the phone a couple of weeks ago.

Soren and Allan were sitting on the exact same spot where we are now enjoying a short rest before the final push towards the summit. Suddenly, they realize that a guide is lowering a client from the steep rock wall, the Upper Moseley Slab, just above the hut. The client lands on his feet not far from them, and only a few seconds later, the guide's cry cuts through the air as he loses his balance and falls off the edge 15 meters above them. He falls only a few meters from Soren and Allan. They do not see where he lands, though; they only hear it! A medicine student, who was also resting at the hut, was lowered down to the guide, but there was nothing he could do.

The Italian guide was experienced and had climbed the Matterhorn 20 times before. Now he was dead!

'It's tough...we gotta be careful,' says Brian in a low voice.

'Absolutely!'

The Upper Moseley Slab is actually a bigger challenge than the slab we have just climbed below the hut. I look at Brian, just to see how he is doing before we move on. For the first time, I notice that he looks a bit tired.

'Are you OK, Brian?'

'Sure, but I can feel that we have been working hard. No worries, though...let's move on,' he replies.

Perhaps I am also tired, but for the moment I only feel the adrenaline that drives me forward and serves as a tremendous help in situations like this. Often it is Brian who finds the extra resources when we are climbing, but it seems as if I have a better day today. As a matter of fact, I cannot remember having felt the combination of good acclimatization, fitness and experience being as perfect as I feel it is today. It is a good feeling. I decide not to ask Brian if he wants to lead but rather take the initiative and set off. I am sure he will make it; Brian is strong.

The Upper Moseley Slab is about as steep as the Moseley Slab, but narrower and therefore easier to overlook: there is only one way – up! For the first time today, we do not have to think about which way to climb. Following the same route as hundreds of other climbers before us, we just climb. Some of them have left pieces of protection on the wall, and I use them to our advantage. It is steep, and we climb on small ledges. I move in deep concentration and take no chances. Almost there!

'OK Brian, you can climb!'

'Climbing!'

I hurry over the edge. The last move is tricky, though, because my foot gets caught in the rope hanging from my harness. Come on! Move, Steffen! I place a sling around a spike in order to belay Brian. I use a carabiner in the sling and tie the rope to it with a Munter Hitch. Perfect! It is as if this knot was designed for the Matterhorn. So simple! Just like that…, and you have made an effective friction device by tying the rope around the carabiner.

As I belay Brian, I see a young girl coming towards us with her guide. I guess the girl is 18 or 19 years old, and she looks tired, but, contrary to the guy we saw earlier, she is still managing to stay collected. I feel happy for her and give her our congratulations; climbing the Matterhorn is a big achievement!

'Wow…it's getting steep now!', says Brian.

'I know. Unfortunately, the fixed ropes don't start until further up,' I answer.

'That is also how I remember it…, but it's nice that so much of the snow has melted,' says Brian.

'True. Let's not put the crampons on just yet...or what do you think?' I laugh. I know all too well that tap-dancing in crampons is not one of Brian's favorites.

'All I have to say is that your stupidity is excused by your mental illness,' Brian snaps, while fighting to hold back the laughter.

We are in familiar terrain: shitty, loose rocks like below the Moseley Slabs. But this section is steeper. It is a mess of towers and boulders garnished by a layer of loose gravel. We see several big blocks that have fallen from somewhere above, and now, as they rest on the gravel, they seem to wait for that small push that will send them surfing off. Terrifying! We move as fast as we can. The adrenalin is still rushing through my body. Move, Steffen! It is as if this intermediate section just needs to be over and done with in order for us to get started on the dreaded fixed ropes further up. No! I cannot allow myself to think this way. Come on! Focus!

In front of me, a giant block cuts off my way ahead. The obvious choice would be to pull myself over it - but that would not be safe. It may only take my weight to get it started. I warn Brian and move further to the right and closer to the ridge.

'I can see the fixed ropes!' I shout to Brian.

'Cool! What does the ground look like?'

'Steep! And endless...The ropes seem to go on forever.'

'Hmm...That's what I thought you'd say.'

'There are also patches of snow on the route from now on...Don't you think we should put on the crampons?' I ask.

'Yeah, this is a good spot,' answers Brian as his eyes search the ground.

‘Save your energy, young man!’ I give the order in my most harsh voice while holding back my laughter.

‘Calm down...one is allowed to find oneself a comfortable seat! I mean, if we really have to put on the devil’s footwear, at least we can relax while doing it, huh?’ Brian replies just as harshly as he looks away to hide his amusement.

High up on the fixed ropes, I can see another team climbing. It is hard, though, to tell if they are going up or coming down. Their progress is slow.

We hurry on. There is still some distance to overcome before we reach the fixed ropes. Luckily, the right way is now straight in front of us: it is a pleasure just to focus on climbing. Along the way, there are some big, twisted iron hoops around which I put the rope for protection. We are doing well. Finally I enjoy being here. The climbing is challenging in some places but does not cause me any problems; we are well acclimatized, and now I’m convinced we will reach the summit. On my right, there is a steep wall. Really steep! Only few places in the world are able to display such impressive, challenging and scary north walls as the Matterhorn which, together with the north faces of the Eiger and the Grandes Jorasses, compose a much desired trilogy for the best and most ambitious alpinists. But even many of these talented climbers have had to give up completing the trilogy due to the difficulties faced on the north wall of the Matterhorn.

There is snow between the boulders and on top of some of them. Not since far below the Solvay Hut has the ridge been as steep as this, and never has it been so exposed. I consider releasing the axe from the clips on my backpack in order to use it to keep my balance. I am in doubt. I know that the axe will be of no use on the fixed ropes, so I scrap the idea and move on as fast as possible. I balance the adrenaline with concentration - one step - balance - another step. Move, Steffen!

'Hey, look at this! The fixed rope is as thick as my wrist.'

'And very smooth,' Brian adds.

'We gotta grab firmly... They are as slippery as soap,' I say as I feel it with my hands.

'Are you leading, then?' suggests Brian.

'OK, but let's agree on how we do this.'

The ropes are fixed to the mountain with big metal loops placed at intervals of 20 to 30 meters. At first, the gradient is not that steep, but it increases to near-vertical further up. We need to make a plan that will work all the way. Time is still important; we simply cannot afford to climb in traditional style with the leader being belayed by the second climber.

'Do you think we can place some protection on the way?' asks Brian.

'I don't know. I don't think so. The surface looks really loose.'

'You're right, but do you remember we talked about using prusiks?'

'Yeah, and I think it is doable, but it will take some time. Let's do it only when necessary.'

'OK. It's your call!'

I look up. Up there, high, high above us, it seems that the ropes continue into the sky. I cannot tell where they end. Still, I have a good feeling. We have trained for this part. This is something we master. We just need to continue like we have done so far: the summit is the goal, but our minds must attend only to the immediate challenge. I look at Brian and our eyes meet. He is focused. We nod to each other and we begin.

Every so often, a shrill sound escapes from my crampon points when they scratch the rock. I move only one arm or foot at a time. My hands move systematically on the rope: a fluid, continuous movement of two hands in a repeated rhythm of holding the rope firmly and letting it go. And then the feet: carefully making sure the crampons hold securely. There are more sounds from the crampons when I slide them further up on the rock, where they are bound to leave scratches. This is my long-lasting contribution to the Matterhorn – a contribution like that of every other climber.

Five meters above me, I spot an anchor. Below me, Brian climbs the section I have just climbed. It looks so steep when I look down towards him. I let my eyes follow the rope across snow, ice, rocks and boulders. Down there, 20 meters below me, I can see Brian's white helmet, his red fleece and his bare hands on the slippery rope. With his body in balance and his head bent forward, he searches for the next secure placement for his crampons.

The iron loop is too thick for me to clip a carabiner around. Instead, I use a short sling and clip our rope onto that. It gives Brian and me a brief moment of rest, but as I climb above this protection, the risk of falling increases further and further. If Brian falls, he will, without a doubt, drag me off the mountain. From where I am now – ten meters above the anchor – I will fall 20 meters and, literally, land on his head. We both know that, and we try not to waste energy worrying about it. I do not monitor Brian's movements, do not think about his climbing and do not feel insecure. I trust him.

By now, I no longer think of the slipperiness of the rope. The climbing is almost mechanical. The voice in my head is still there, however: focus! Move, Steffen!

In front of me is another iron loop. It only takes little imagination to see it as a meat hook. Forget it! I put the rope through it and climb onwards. There is snow everywhere now. In some places, the fixed rope is a bit icy, but it does not cause me any problems. The rhythm of my movement is constant and careful. I kick small steps in the packed snow with my crampons to get their points to bite securely.

'Rooooock! Look out, Briaaan!'

I press my body into the wall as several rocks fly by me. Someone above us has started a minor rockfall. The biggest rocks are the size of a child's head. I try to take cover and pull my shoulders up to my ears. It is raining rocks, but luckily only a small stone hits my helmet - but what about Brian? Is he hit?

'Are you OK, Steffen?' he shouts when the silence has returned.

'Yeah, and you?'

'I'm fine...let's get a move on!'

I hurry upwards. Above me, I can see a team coming down. They are probably tired and therefore perhaps not concentrating as much as they should. I must pay full attention! I'm 20 meters above the last anchor. My mind is swept clean of irrational thoughts. Three meters to the next anchor! That's all.

I quickly clip the sling I always wear tied to my harness to the anchor. I belay Brian. I could continue, but after more than a hundred meters of hanging by the arms, I am sure a short break will do us good. I look down the Hörnli Ridge. What a view: even if we are still some hundred meters or so below the summit, it seems as if the rest of the world is below us. I can see all the way to Zermatt and further down the valley.

'Hey Brian...welcome to the Matterhorn,' I say laughing as I pass him a sling to clip into for safety.

'Cheers!'

'I just thought we should stand here for a while,' I joke, as I prepare to move on.

'That's fine! And hey...check the weather, Steffen. Is it perfect or what?'

'It sure is. We're lucky.'

I leave Brian, and being belayed by him off the anchor, I continue the climb. I look at him and smile. I feel great. Now we will make it to the summit. Technically, the route is straightforward but, climbing it is definitely not something you just do. My focus is undiminished, but I cannot avoid some feeling of joy. I feel privileged.

We have not seen the summit for some time, and this must be the last fixed rope. Soon, I will climb past the end of this steep section and onto 'the Roof' from where I will be able to see the summit again. The Roof is the less steep part of the mountain just below the summit. This is where the near-vertical wall changes to a slab and where a long line of metal rings will offer us protection the rest of the way.

I look to the right. Somewhere out there it all ended for Croz, Hadow, Hudson and Douglas. I feel as if I am climbing in the middle of a history book. This is not a story or a picture. This is reality. Right here, the adventure came to a fatal end for the four climbers who, one hour earlier, had been standing on the summit of the Matterhorn as the first men ever.

The Roof is less steep. Still, it is challenging enough as the last days' snowfall has covered most of the rock and hidden all the holds. I secure myself to the first anchor and belay Brian as he climbs up to me. Several climbing teams are descending towards us along the very same line we are using for our ascent. So far, we have not needed our axes, but now they will be of use. I carefully take off my pack and loosen the loops that have kept the axe in place until now.

'Do you want some water?' I ask Brian and hand him my bottle.

'Thanks! What's the strategy from here...do you think we can manage with running belays?'

'I certainly think we should try...but I'm going to need both ice screws,' I reply.

'Of course, here you are!'

'But Brian, if I run out of screws, I might traverse out to the rocks to put in some protection,' I say as I point to the edge on the left where small pieces of rock are sticking out of the snow.

'Good idea. It's definitely not a place to climb with no protection at all.'

'No, that would be stupid.'

'Indeed,' says Brian, and he continues, 'if we start sliding here, we won't stop before we are back at the bloody campsite.'

We decide to continue keeping the relatively large distance we have had between us so far. In this way, we can climb further on fewer pieces of protection. The Roof is mainly hard ice, which makes it unlikely that we will be using our snow anchor, which requires soft snow. There are a couple of iron hooks sticking through the snow, and we might be able to use the few free standing boulders as anchors. There is no more fixed rope; from this point on we only have our axes.

I move quickly towards the next iron hook.

'Five meters!' shouts Brian.

'OK!'

Shit! The next anchor is at least eight meters away. I will have to put in some protection – the alternative is to climb without any protection at all when Brian runs out of rope. I test the ice with my axe. It seems all right. I scrape away the snow and find a good ice surface beneath. I place a screw.

'On belay!' I shout to Brian

'Climbing!'

A bit further up, I place a sling around the iron hook and move on as quickly as possible. From here, I cannot see the next anchor, but I assume it is hidden behind the small group of climbers standing 25 meters above me. I move towards them.

Ten meters before the anchor, I place another ice screw. As I look up, a guide starts lowering his client down the mountain - right towards me!

'Hey, could you please wait a second?' I shout to the guide.

I have tried this too many times. A couple of years ago, it almost resulted in an accident in Chamonix where an American, coming down the mountain we were climbing, continued directly into me and pushed me out of balance. I had to struggle hard to stay on the mountain. In situations like this, I now have a clear strategy: if it does not work when I ask nicely, I shout, and if that does not help, I shout louder. Not to be a wise guy or because I think it is my right more than theirs, but simply to avoid either of us getting h urt.

The guide above me pretends he has not heard me.

'Hey you..., he can't see me... You gotta stop!' I shout – and so loud that the entire mountain can hear me.

'No, it's all right,' the guide replies.

No way, it is not all right. But the guide continues lowering his client, who is now only a few meters above my head. The client does not respond, neither to my shouting nor to the instructions from his guide, and so I brace myself.

I shout out again and try to warn the client, but apparently nothing gets through to him. I put my hands in front of me, and when he is half a step away, I gently push him to the right. He stares at me in a daze and looks as if he has no idea about what is going on around him. Scary!

I suddenly realize that I have forgotten to warn Brian. I turn around to signal that we must protect the rope from the crampons of the descending climber. But Brian has got it all under control: he has seen it all and is already trying to swing the rope to the left and away from the danger zone. I climb on and tie into the same anchor the guide is using. I refrain from commenting on the situation since the danger is over.

From here, I belay Brian. I might be able to continue without the ice screws, but it is not worth running the risk. I wait and look at the sky. It is still nice and clear, but a few clouds are approaching from the southeast.

'So Kjaer, are you making new acquaintances?' asks Brian, while attaching his sling to the anchor.

'Yeah, but they didn't want to play ball with a guy like me,' I answer as I try to find a grimace which shows a little contempt.

'Hmm...hard to understand,' Brian mumbles sarcastically.

So typical of him, and so cool! He may be tired, but I think it is tough that he is able to recognize his condition without surrendering to it. For most people, acknowledging their situation will also accelerate it. For example, if you start feeling tired, the sensation will increase, and if you feel scared, you will be frightened about being scared, and in that way, the situation quickly escalates to something hard to control. For Brian, it is different; he knows himself and his body. He knows he gets tired and he knows he gets scared. And that is exactly why it does not frighten him. It only makes him pay more attention to what he is doing.

Three Italians are passing us as they are descending. We have not seen them before; they were not at the hut last night. I assume they have climbed the mountain from the Italian side. Maybe they have used the Southwest Ridge or the Lion Ridge as it is named because of a lion-like rock formation further down. We congratulate them and continue towards the summit.

I can now see the statue of Saint Bernard, which is placed close to the summit. Well protected by the rocks behind his back, this guardian angel of the mountain watches over us. At least according to the Catholics who believe that every person has his or her own guardian angel which, on behalf of God, accompanies us. St. Bernard is ours; the guardian angel of mountaineers.

Saint Bernard was a Christian priest who lived from 923 to 1008. Among other things, he founded a hospice for mountain travelers and, of course, it was after him the enormous rescue dog was named: the Saint Bernard race was originally used to dig out people caught in the snow by avalanches.

Saint Bernard was canonized in 1115 and has been a saint ever since. Now he stands here as a bronze statue bolted to the Matterhorn. He probably never imagined that he would be used as the final anchor point on the last pitch of the Matterhorn. But that is how it is: around the waist of the statue, a vast number of slings and rope loops are tied, and in that way he also serves a very practical purpose. Probably just in the spirit of the old saint. Thanks, Saint Bernard!

I smile, slightly embarrassed, as I tie my sling to the waist of the saint to use it to belay Brian. I can hardly wait to show it to him.

'Say hello to Saint Bernard, Brian!'

'Hmmm!'

'No, hello!'

'Hmmm!'

I know; Brian thinks that this kind of fooling around is close to blasphemy, so I leave it. Instead, I turn my attention to the final steps. From here, there are only 25 meters to the summit. It is an easy traverse on a snowy track. It is, however, also one of the more airy ones...to the left, down towards Italy, it is almost a free fall.

'Do you wanna go first, Brian?' I ask.

'No no, this summit's yours, Kjaer..., get going!'

With small steps I approach the summit. This is huge. Fantastic!Focus, Steffen. Concentrate, all the way! One more step. I look at the summit. The last meters are slightly steeper. I lean on my axe and look back at Brian. I smile at him and take the last steps.

'This is the summit...I'm on the summit, Brian.'

'All right, all right, I hear you,' he laughs back.

'I'm on the summit of the Matterhorn...come on!'

This is the summit, I repeat to myself and feel enormously proud. I am not totally satisfied: I am far from down and safe, but I am proud. Proud of myself. Proud of Brian. Of us!

I grab the rope and take it in as Brian takes his last steps to the summit.

'Damn, Brian...congratulations!'

'Thanks, and the same to you Kjaer. Well done!'

'Thanks, but I think you may have to be the leader going down,' I reply.

‘No problem.’

‘Look at that, we can see Mont Blanc.’

‘Yes, but we’re here...and this is so much bigger to me,’ says Brian.

‘Same for me...it’s amazing!’

‘It is. Photo’s Kjaer! We must have summit shots!’

‘Most certainly, but first I need to see the panorama, Jorgensen!’

‘You do that, but be careful now,’ laughs Brian.

I spread out my arms and begin ever so slowly and carefully. With my arms spread out, I allow the euphoria, the joy and the pride to turn me around as the most beautiful panoramic view passes before my eyes. I am struck, struck by the greatest sensation to be found.

An Historic Evacuation

In the peak season, rescue operations are an inevitable part of daily life on the Matterhorn. The Swiss helicopter company Air Zermatt is known far beyond the Swiss borders for its performance and excellent results in the many, often spectacular, rescue operations in the mountains.

When the sun rose on July 15th, 2003, none of the estimated 90 climbers on the Hörnli Ridge knew that they were going to be part of a rescue operation that would become known throughout the world.

At 10.30 am, the Zermatt mountain guide Gianni Mazzone was climbing a couple of hundred meters above the Hörnli Hut when he felt the mountain shake under his feet. He ran upwards as fast as he could and just managed to avoid the rock slide and thus the hundreds of cubic meters of rock, which suddenly came rushing down. Gianni Mazzone immediately called the rescue service and told them that none of the climbers located above the giant rock slide would be able to climb down through the now very dangerous terrain without running extreme risks. This started a rescue operation of unprecedented proportions; one that would make a chapter of its own in the history of the Matterhorn.

The operation on the mountain was led by the experienced manager of the rescue service, Bruno Jelk. He coordinated the four-hour-long helicopter evacuation during which the pilots, Fabian Zuber and Gerald Biner, flew a shuttle service to bring down the climbers. For some of these climbers, it must have been a thrilling experience; for others, it must have been nerve wracking to be hanging in groups of four on a long wire 30 meters below the helicopters. Miraculously, no one was hurt.

During the following days, the mountain was closed for all climbers in order for experts to determine the safety condition of the mountain. Using different types of aids, the experts carried out a number of analyses and made measurements to find out if the Matterhorn had settled again.

After the incident, geologists explained that the enormous slide might have been caused by diminishing permafrost, which normally keeps the mountain together. The mountain was literally melting due to the unusually high temperatures during spring and summer.

In the media, the drama on the Matterhorn was a great story. In the days following the rock slide, newspapers around the world had articles about the Matterhorn, and soon the many inexperienced mountaineers, who venture out to climb it every day, became a dominating theme. Some newspapers described the Matterhorn as an easily climbed mountain; one newspaper even quoted a climber for saying that 'even a cow can climb the Matterhorn'. Such statements naturally worried the rescue service.

Every year, they have about 1500 operations in the Alps, and on average, there is one per day on the Matterhorn alone.

Churchill – The Price-conscious Climber

Theodore Roosevelt was not the only famous statesman to spend his youth climbing mountains in the Zermatt area. Winston Churchill (1874-1965), the English Prime Minister to be, (1940-1945 and 1951-1955), also took up the challenge of mountaineering.

When Winston Churchill took office for the first time in 1940, he stated that he could not promise the English people anything but 'blood, toil, tears and sweat'. And who knows, perhaps he had come to know this side of himself in the mountains around Zermatt.

The story has it that Churchill had planned to climb the Matterhorn but changed his mind and set out to climb the difficult Monte Rosa at 4634 meters instead. Even if this was no easy mountain, the guide only charged half the price to guide Churchill compared to what he charged for the Matterhorn. This was a saving Churchill could not resist.

The Accident

Monday, July 7th

'This is huge, Brian.'

'I know. Unbelievable!'

We are alone on the summit. Brian and I. Around us we have everything it takes to make it a real summit, which is not really a lot: just the fresh, clean air as it can only be experienced from the top of a mountain, few clouds and a fantastic view. Everything else is below us.

'This time we have a perfect summit with a perfect view,' says Brian, referring to the cloudy summits of last week.

'We certainly do...it's such an amazing view.'

In reality, I suppose that the views from other summits are just as impressive as the one we are experiencing right now on the Matterhorn. But this is our present reality; reduced to the dreams and the pride - and we are standing amidst both. We stand on the summit of the Matterhorn: this is our entire world and life at this moment in time. It is so perfect. Exactly as we have dreamed it would be.

You are only halfway, Steffen, remember that! Euphoria is slowly replaced by the reality of our situation. We have been on the summit for ten minutes, and it has been fantastic to allow myself to release my happiness, to be proud, to thoroughly enjoy everything around me and see Brian forget his weariness. But now my focus is coming back. Focus! The voice in my head reminds me that we are only halfway on this expedition. If it had not been mountaineering, had we instead won a soccer match or reached the goal of our careers, or had we experienced this enormous satisfaction anywhere else, we probably would have partied on. But this is mountaineering. We are on the summit of the Matterhorn: the mountain that has claimed more lives through history than any other – and most of them have happened on the way down.

It is 11.45 am. The altimeter says 4478 meters. I let my eyes pan the horizon one last time while I prepare a small ball of snuff and place it under my upper lip. Brian is chewing on one of his dry cakes, and with the back of his hand he wipes away the crumbs. Or is it the smile? I sense that he is thinking about the descent.

'What do you say, Steffen...shall we?'

'Sure, let's get down!'

As Brian walks back towards the statue of Saint Bernard, I carefully monitor his every movement. It is completely impossible to belay him from here; it is all loose rock and snow. Hence, my task is simple and well defined: should Brian stumble and fall to one side, I would have to jump to the other side to create a counterweight to stop his fall.

At the statue, Brian clips into Mr. Bernard's waist belt and belays me with a Munter Hitch. Approaching Brian, I take a look at the Roof, which we now have to pass. I smile as I remember Brian stating that a fall would not stop before we reached our tent on the campsite in Zermatt. He is probably right. We decide to abseil from anchor to anchor. The solid iron rings are placed at an interval of 20 to 30 meters. We could have saved a lot of time if we had carried two ropes, but we did not. Instead, we can only abseil half the length of the rope at a time – roughly the distance between the rings.

'If we just had another rope, the descent would have been so much faster. This is gonna take forever!' I complain.

'I know, but on the other hand, we would have had to carry it up here.'

'You're right...this is probably the better solution,' I say while I pull half of the rope through the belt on the statue.

When Brian puts the rope through his figure-of-8, I remember an incident from our first ice climbing trip to Hemsedal in Norway. We were preparing for an abseil and it was freezing. The big gloves did not make handling the equipment any easier, and as Brian put the rope through his figure-of-8, he dropped it. Before we were able to do anything, the device slid away on the frozen snow. We followed it with our eyes until it found a hole in the snow through which it disappeared. We heard it hit rocks on the way down until it came to rest at the bottom many meters below. Brian was furious; it actually ruined most of his day. The problem was not that he had to buy a new one; to Brian, the problem was that he had not been careful enough and therefore had lost something of importance for our safety. One week later, I gave him a new one for his birthday, and I know he dares not drop that one. That day we both learned a lesson.

'I'm out!' shouts Brian.

'OK!'

We begin what seems like an endless series of abseils. I thread my figure-of-8, check it and start lowering myself down the mountain, down towards Brian, who is already preparing for the next abseil.

'Here...clip into this,' says Brian as he hands me a yellow sling he has tied to the iron ring.

I quickly secure myself so that I can release the rope. Brian is already waiting to pull the rope down from the anchor above me, and the very instant I let go, he starts pulling. I make sure that the rope passes through the ring so we can continue immediately when the rope is down.

'Rope!' shouts Brian.

I coil the two halves of the rope after tying the ends together and throw it in the direction of the next anchor. We have done this a hundred times before. Brian links up and begins the next abseil. I detect no tiredness; apparently the summit has refueled him. Super! Abseil upon abseil – it is almost mechanical. At the anchors, we work quickly and efficiently, and not until one of us begins lowering himself, do we find the time for a sarcastic comment, which is instantly returned. Then we laugh and move on.

It has been a while since we have seen other climbers. In a south easterly direction, I spot a glider between two layers of cloud. Far, far below us, sun rays reach the glacier. It is all part of the breathtaking experience. To some, it would probably be extremely anxiety provoking to find themselves in a situation which seems so far from the comfortable and safe life they know. From a psychological point of view, the mountaineer often finds himself in stressful situations when he climbs up a mountain side or crosses a treacherous crevasse. In a civilized everyday life, we do what we can to arrange our lives to be as undemanding as possible. In other words, we place ourselves in the comfort zone, but unfortunately, by doing so, we cut ourselves off from a range of interesting and inspiring experiences that might yield insight as well as personal development. I know that mountaineering is by no means the answer to all problems, but still I claim that the mountains and a stay in this magnificent classroom can teach us more about handling stress than coaches who operate in comfortable conference rooms with fancy powerpoint presentations are able to.

For four years I worked as a human resource manager in a successful team building company. I taught the managers corporate skills based on outdoor training. It centered on strengthening personal insight as a means of enhancing the potential for communication and cooperation.

It was important that it took place in an unfamiliar environment due to the simple fact that it is hard to facilitate personal development and change if people are positioned in their comfort zone. Most of our courses therefore took place in the woods or by the sea and typically had elements of climbing and water activities. All these exercises gave the participants the opportunity to learn that their stress threshold was lower and their co-operative abilities limited when acting in unknown terrain. This is exactly why it is a really good idea to seek such situations – to create the opportunity for gaining insight and for development. Of course, it should be done under controlled circumstances and under conditions allowing oneself or the instructor to ensure safety.

‘What’s on your mind, Steffen?’ questions Brian as he pulls down the rope from the last abseil on the Roof.

‘Not much...just how privileged we are...experiencing all this.’

‘What do you mean?’

‘The mountain..., the summit..., all of it...and happiness, perhaps.’

‘Don’t go soft on me here at 4200 meters, Kjaer... We have to get down, you know,’ laughs Brian.

‘I suppose so,’ I say silently, trying to avoid his eyes.

But I cannot avoid it – our eyes meet and we crack up. This is so cool. In some way, Brian is an important part of my comfort zone, just as I guess I am part of his.

‘Rope!’ shouts Brian.

‘K-pech!’ The rope snaps every time it whirls through the air and hits the wall. Brian clips in his figure-of-8 and off he goes. Perhaps we could have used the fixed ropes. The numerous abseils undoubtedly take more time, but it is much safer than clambering down the thick slippery ropes.

I have lost count of the number of abseils we have made since we left the summit. Maybe ten. Maybe twelve. We have stopped wasting time on considering whether it is worthwhile abseiling; mechanically, we just move on from abseil to abseil.

‘What time is it?’ asks Brian as we reach the Solvay Hut and take a break.

'Half past four...we are a little late.'

'I know. Maybe we did too many abseils. But don't you think we'll get down before dark?'

'Probably, just about.'

'Do you want a cake?' Brian offers me one while he struggles to keep the dry crumbs inside his mouth.

We have just abseiled the Upper Moseley Slab from exactly the point where the Italian guide fell to his death a few years ago. Now we have only the lower Moseley Slab left before we can tie into the rope and start climbing down the ridge.

'It's so peaceful here,' says Brian.

'It is. Do you want to take a look inside the hut?'

'Why not...But it has to be a short one; we must get going soon.'

From the outside, the hut appears warm and attractive with its stylish wooden walls and solar panels. The inside arrangements are limited, though, to say the least. There are bunks with dark blue mattresses – that is it. On the wall hangs the emergency radio. We share a bottle of water while we pack: crampons and ice screws will not be of much use, and they are packed at the bottom. I check my headlamp and place my remaining water reserves on top of it all.

'Right! Let's go!'

We leave the Solvay Hut and balance our way along the ridge until we reach the Moseley Slab. Here, we abseil once again. A couple of hundred meters below, I can see a team coming up, probably to spend the night in the hut.

It is now a couple of hours since we left the hut. So far, it has been almost as hard finding the way down as it was coming up. This is not like any other climb where the descent is a simple thing that has to be done. This is the Matterhorn! We climb up and down and up again; we slide on the loose gravel while doing what we can to avoid loose rocks and boulders ready to surf off. On the most difficult passages, we place protection. I am in front and Brian is behind with his firm attention on the rope – ready to hold me if I slip on the loose surface. This does not feel safe at all: the excess energy I felt when we ascended the mountain is gone and has been replaced by a limited focus on my next movement. Though the climbing is not difficult, I can feel the effect of a long day's hard work: for the first time today, I feel tired.

'I am getting tired,' I inform Brian as he hands me the climbing gear he has removed.

'Do you want a break?'

'That won't be necessary...I can still climb. I just feel that it's getting harder to stay focused.'

'Here...have some water.'

'Cheers. Do you recognize this section?' I ask.

'I'm not sure, but on the rock to the left there is some fixed gear which at least indicates that we're on the right route.'

'Cool...but we must be careful now, Brian. We are tired...we must stay alert. We had better take an extra break then.'

'OK!'

BOOM! There is a huge bang. Further out on the east side we see another one of the Matterhorn's infamous rockfalls. Boulders the size of fridges are tumbling down the mountain. I shiver. Focus, Steffen!

We continue along a small rock wall while I follow the rockfall as it disappears down towards the glacier. That is probably also where we will end if we fall here. Don't think about it!

'I'm removing the last piece of gear...is it possible for you to place something?' asks Brian.

'Just a moment..., mmm... No..., in a few meters, perhaps.'

'OK, but then we'll be moving without any anchors.'

'All right. We really have to be careful here.'

On my right, there is a drop to the glacier, and in front of me, a steep wall rises. We either have to go back to see if there is another way or try to climb the wall to the left.

'Brian, I can try climbing to the top of the wall,' I suggest as I point upwards.

'OK, but do you think this is right?'

'I'm not sure... most likely we can abseil down on the other side.'

'Fine! I'll follow when there is no more rope.'

'Good. Give me the gear, and I'll place some protection where I possibly can.'

The wall is steep but relatively easy to climb. For a second, my mind is in Sweden, on Kullaberg, where the rock is also quite loose. I test the holds by knocking on them. If they respond with a hollow sound, it is a no-go. I look for a crack in which to place protection but it is impossible. Instead, I concentrate on the climbing and try to put as little weight on the holds as possible.

'Two more meters and then I'm up!'

'Excellent!'

'But don't climb just yet. Let me check the other side first.'

'OK!'

At the top, I reach a small plateau. Immediately, I see that we definitely should not go that way. But at the other end to the right, I see a sling. Well, at least we are not stranded.

'OK, Brian, I think we can get down on the other side, but there is not enough rope for me to check it...and I can't place any protection right away.'

'Copy that!'

'But you may climb!'

'Climbing!'

The rope is stretched out between us, but when Brian climbs, it slackens and so allows me to try to find a place to put in some protection.

BANG! The crash from below makes me instinctively throw my body down on the rock in front of me. I land hard on my stomach. Just as my fingers grip on to the edge of the rock, I feel an extreme pull on my harness.

I am fighting to hold on. It feels as if the rope is tearing me apart. Don't let go, damn it! My fingers slip a few millimeters. Don't let go, Steffen! I am holding on with only the tip of my fingers now. The rope is cutting into my left leg. Fight! It feels like an eternity. I am desperately trying to maintain my grip on the rock; I just hope I have the strength to endure.

Then it eases; it is still tight, but the fight is over. I no longer need to struggle to hold on. Everything is quiet. There is not a sound. I do not know why I do not say anything; I just cannot. I am confused. A thousand thoughts race through my mind, yet

I think of nothing. I have never felt such an alarming silence. I cannot bring a sound to my lips. I just hold on to the rock; I can hardly believe it is over.

'Are you all right, Steffen?'

'Yes, I am,' I manage to utter, after some hesitation.

Why does he ask me if I am all right? If nothing has happened to him, then what on earth was that?

'What about you...are you OK?' I finally manage to ask.

'My foot hurts, but I don't think it is anything serious.'

'But where are you?'

'At the foot of the wall, I am standing on the gravel.'

'But why's the rope so tight? Damn, I feel as if I'm being torn in two!' I say, exaggerating a bit.

'I don't know. There's a bit of slack down here.'

This is weird. It certainly feels like there is something heavy on the other end of the rope. I am still lying on my belly trying to figure out what just happened. Slowly, I loosen my grip and move in the direction of the rope one inch at a time. I feel the pull easing. Now I see that the rope is jammed between the wall and a boulder resting against the wall. We have been lucky. This may have saved our lives.

Below me, I see Brian waiting by a boulder the size of a cooker. I can tell he is in pain.

'How bad is it?' I ask.

'It's probably just the numbness from the impact,' he replies, while trying not to put weight on his left foot.

'Are you able to climb?'

‘Yeah...let’s get on with it.’

‘Are you sure?...You have to be bloody well sure, Jorgensen! If you are not, we’ll have to call a chopper,’ I say, and wonder how on earth I am supposed to get us down from the mountain if he cannot walk.

‘It’ll be alright. Just give me a second.’

‘OK, but let me know if it’s not working out, right?’

‘Sure. I will.’

‘Hold on and let me set up a belay.‘

I untie myself to get enough rope to be able to belay Brian. At the other side of the plateau, I place a sling around a boulder and clip the rope into it. While Brian is climbing, I look around and try to plan how to move on.

He is coming closer. So he can still climb. He is even keeping a good pace.

I am re-focused. The shock is gone, and I concentrate completely on making the right decisions.

‘How are you?’ I ask as he pokes his head over the edge.

‘I am fine. It’ll be alright,’ he answers.

I look him in the eyes and repeat my proposal about a helicopter, but Brian does not think it is necessary. The deal is clear: we have to be honest about what we can and cannot do. I am sure he will be. The question is what it takes for Brian to make that decision. I know him well enough to know that he is capable of mobilizing enormous resources when the going gets tough. Determination is one of these resources, but pride may be another one.

I ask Brian to untie himself from the rope so I can prepare an anchor for our abseil. This time, I do not ask his opinion; I only tell him what to do. I am one hundred percent aware of my responsibility. The initiative is mine alone to take from now on.

'What happened?' I ask while going through my slings in search of an old one to leave behind.

'It's so bloody stupid.... Apparently, I misjudged the rock; I didn't see it was loose. It seemed all right, but when I pulled myself up, it came loose and flew right at me.'

'The one you were standing by when I saw you?' I ask and recall the image of the cooker-sized boulder.

'Yeah.'

'How high up were you when it happened?'

'About one and a half meters, I think.'

'Then what?'

'Well, I'm falling, and, at the same time, I see four or five big rocks fall right at me... They must have come loose together with the boulder..., but just before they hit me, the rope tightens and makes me swing a bit to the right...just enough to make the rocks pass by me – except for one, which grazes my arm.

'No shit?!?'

'Yeah, and then, exactly at the same moment I reach the ground, that bloody boulder lands on my foot.'

'So that's what I heard! What happened then?' I ask and shiver.

'Well, fortunately the gravel was loose enough for me to pull my foot out, and, luckily, I didn't fall down the slope because the rope was taut when I reached the ground – was that you?'

'Yes. I heard the rocks fall, and I threw myself down on that rock over there and held on to it with all I had!' I say and continue in a lower voice: 'I thought I was being split in two.'

'We have been lucky,' says Brian.

'That we have...maybe we should send a prayer to Saint Bernard,' I answer and smile as I prepare our abseil.

I can tell the old sling has been here for some years. The colors have faded and there is obvious damage from previous use. I replace it with one of my own. It is going to be an exposed abseil. The wall below us forms a vertical corner that is completely polished. It ends on a small shelf from where we have another one or two abseils before we are down.

I look at Brian. What would have happened if I had not managed to hold on to the rock? What would have happened had the rope not got jammed? And what if..? I cannot think these questions through, and I certainly cannot allow myself to spend energy on doing so. Focus!

I approach the edge and look over my shoulder. I check the figure-of-8 again. Just as I start my abseil, I come to think that maybe I should have sent Brian down first. It is too late. I pull myself back a bit, just enough to look him in the eyes.

'Brian, are you sure you can do it?'

'Yes. Go on now.'

'OK, but be careful.'

'I will.'

‘Listen, Brian..., whatever you normally double check, check it an extra time now. You may be a bit..., you know..., considering what you’ve just experienced and all...So check it three times, OK?’

‘Of course,’ he replies.

I lean out and let the rope carry my weight. I look at Brian one last time and abseil down the steep wall, which turns out to be overhanging. I realize that it may be quite difficult to land on the shelf below me, and suddenly I am pleased that I went first. In this way, I can pull Brian onto the shelf. I estimate the abseil to be 15, maybe 20, meters. The shelf is about one meter wide all the way along the wall. It feels safe. I quickly get off the rope and immediately start to look for a new anchor for the next abseil. There is one five meters from me. Even if the shelf is narrower over there, it is our best shot.

I watch Brian abseiling. It does not look good. He hardly uses his left foot. He lowers himself slowly while trying to balance by using his right foot.

‘How’s it going?’ I ask when he is about five meters from the shelf.

‘I’ll manage.’

‘Which foot was it again?’ I ask stupidly.

‘LEFT!’

It was a silly remark. It is obvious that he cannot use his left foot. Maybe I just asked to gain some time. But there is no choice: I am unable to get us both down safely. Or maybe I can? I am still in doubt. Will he be able to hold me if I slip or fall? And what will happen when it gets dark? For how long can he continue? I have to make up my mind.

What the hell did we have to come down here for? Why did we leave the plateau from which a helicopter could have picked us up easily? I am annoyed with myself that I could not make the right decision up there.

'Sit down over here, Brian,' I say, and help him find something to lean against.

'Right.'

'Brian, listen...I have decided to call a helicopter. This is not going to work...It's not safe to continue like this.'

'OK...no problem.'

I open my backpack and find my mobile phone. I wonder how the rescue team is going to find us. We do not know exactly where we are. I give Brian my water bottle. He has got an empty look in his eyes, a sort of resignation. This is the right thing to do. Now I am certain.

'How are we going to tell them where we are?' I ask without really expecting an answer.

'Use your altimeter...that should help them.'

Of course! Why did I not think of that? My watch tells me that we are situated at 3765 meters. The phone number I know by heart: 144.

'Hello...is this the mountain rescue service?' I ask when someone says something in German at the other end of the line.

'Yes, this is mountain rescue. How can I help you?'

'Thanks...we've had an accident on the Matterhorn, and now we need your assistance.'

'All right, what happened?'

'My partner fell from a rock face and hurt his foot...it might be broken.'

'OK. How many are you?'

'Just the two of us.'

'OK. And where are you?'

'It's a bit difficult to tell...but on the Hörnli Ridge. Altitude: 3 – 7 – 6 – 5...'

'3-7-6-5...on the Hörnli Ridge?'

'Yes. I will be waving a yellow jacket when I see you.'

'OK. We will come and get you.'

I look down to Zermatt and try to imagine how long it will take for them to arrive.

'What did they say?' asks Brian.

'They will come right away.'

'Do you think they'll use a line? I mean, it's not that easy to get to us here by helicopter.

'They probably will,' I answer, and start pulling down the rope while I try not to worry.

I am very annoyed that we did not stay on the plateau. This shelf is probably one of the most difficult places on all of the Matterhorn for a helicopter rescue. I know that time is working against us. It is already 8.10 pm, and in one hour it will be dark. It is of no use thinking more about the accident or the decisions made; I have to focus on helping Brian as much as possible. I definitely have to make sure that I don't contribute to his feeling of guilt. I am very sure that he is already blaming himself big time.

'Look out, Brian, the rope is coming down!'

'Yes, OK...but, Steffen, it was such a small thing, just a tiny little error, and we have been through it already! Damn, it's so stupid!'

'What's done is done, Brian, don't blame yourself...it could just as easily have been...'

'I know, it's just...'

'Do you want something to eat?' I ask.

'Just water, thanks. Do you think they'll use our own harnesses?'

'Good question. I don't know. What else can they do?'

'I know. I know that's what they did with the Italian guide, but of course, he was already dead,' says Brian in a dry way so characteristic of his sense of humor.

Chop, chop, chop...the well-known sound of a helicopter approaches. I called them only 20 minutes ago, but I can already see the rescue helicopter hovering over the Hörnli Hut. Now, it seems they are flying directly at us – and they are going fast. I am waving my jacket above my head. Have they seen us? The helicopter maintains its course. I wave the jacket again. They are now so close that I can see the crew through the front window. I curl up the jacket and raise both arms above my head. At a distance, I now look like a giant Y; the international sign for "we need help!"

The helicopter hovers over us for a moment. Then it flies away, back towards Zermatt where it came from.

'They did see us, didn't they?' asks Brian.

'I am sure they did.'

'Hmm...maybe they need backup?'

We can see the helicopter landing at the Hörnli Hut. It is getting dark.

'Our Irish friends are probably getting nervous...we told them we'd be down by now,' says Brian.

'You're right. I'll find them as soon as we get down.'

'Do you think they will take us both to Zermatt?'

'If they have room; otherwise, I'll walk back tomorrow. It's no problem.'

Chop, chop, chop; the helicopter is returning.

'Look! There is someone hanging from under it!' says Brian as he points in the direction of the helicopter.

'Yep...and soon that will be you, Brian,' I laugh.

'Cool,' he answers, impressed.

The line is probably 30 meters long. At the end of it, a member of the rescue team is hanging in a harness with his equipment in his backpack and a helmet on his head. An intercom is mounted on the helmet. The down force from the blades of the helicopter is so powerful that I have to sit down to avoid being blown off the shelf. It is hovering right above us. The rescuer is swaying back and forth, and he continuously speaks in his intercom to coordinate his landing. I hold on to Brian with one arm, and with the other I pull in the rescuer. The man releases himself from the line and informs the pilot that he is off. He repeats it and the helicopter flies away, some hundred meters or so in the direction of the Hörnli Hut.

The noise from the helicopter is still so loud that I cannot hear what Brian and the rescuer are talking about, but I can see what is going on: Brian points to his foot and the rescuer says something. He then points to Brian's harness and receives a clear nod from my defeated partner. The rescuer takes a closer look at the harness and clips in one of his steel carabiners. In the carabiner he also places a yellow sling, and he then calls for the helicopter. So far, I have not talked to him, and I do not know what he and Brian have talked about, so I have no idea where they are taking him.

'See you, Brian!' I shout.

'Yeah, see you!'

The rescuer connects the yellow sling to the line and gives instructions through the intercom. The helicopter takes off. At first, just a little bit and then a little bit more. Brian is hanging right in front of me. I hope he will enjoy the evening sky over the mountain tops if nothing else.

'All right, so what's next? Will the chopper come back for you and me?' I ask the rescue guy as Brian is disappearing; he is hanging some 300 meters above the Matterhorn's terrifying east wall.

'Yes. They'll come back.'

'OK. Is it able to carry both of us at the same time?' I ask somewhat worried that the approaching darkness will forbid anyone being taken out by helicopter.

'Yes...that's no problem,' he replies. He is not the talkative type.

From his backpack he takes out another yellow sling that almost looks like an octopus with six arms. The top point will be fastened to the line, and the weight is placed in each of the loops. He asks about my harness and clips me into one of the loops. He clips himself into another loop and does the same to the three backpacks. And here we are: on a small shelf on the Matterhorn, tied tightly together with backpacks hanging around our legs. Waiting.

It is a strange feeling being lifted off the mountain in this way. Since 4.15 am this morning, I have been thinking about my every movement. Before every step, I have looked critically at what I was going to step onto, I have evaluated every hold and double-checked every gear placement. My senses have been on high alert, and only in a few instances have I allowed unnecessary thoughts to disturb my concentration. I get a strange sensation in my stomach as the chopper takes off and our feet are lifted off the shelf which has been our safe post for the last hour or so. Perhaps I also feel the adrenaline level dropping.

The rescuer directs the pilot - five meters - three meters - two meters - one meter. We are down. He disconnects us from the line and signals to the pilot that he is clear to go. Brian has been placed ten meters away from us, where he is lying half in pain and half flirting with a nurse in climbing gear. A very pretty nurse, too.

It is hard to tell how many are involved in the operation. Other than the rescuer and the nurse, there are the pilot and another two rescue team members. They have probably been waiting here at the hut after they flew up to us the second time. Another helicopter is approaching.

'Do you want to stay, or do you want a lift to town?' asks the pilot as I am taking off my harness and all the other gear.

'To the town? You mean Zermatt?' I ask.

'Yes. You can fly with me to Zermatt if you like,' the kind pilot offers.

'Thanks... That would be fine!'

'All right. Then you have two minutes to get your stuff from the hut.'

'OK..., thanks.'

All this is going on only some ten meters from the Hörnli Hut, and we are not alone. By the hut wall, every climber in the hut is watching. I do not blame them for their curiosity. Had this happened yesterday, I would have done the same – with camera and all. But it would have made me think the same as I can see they are thinking now. In a few hours, they are going to climb the Matterhorn. Now they have seen how our adventure ended.

I hurry to find the small plastic boxes with our excess equipment and throw it in my backpack. The guardian at the reception has already found our membership cards from the Danish Mountaineering Council, which we gave him yesterday. He hands me a small piece of paper. I wonder what it is as I unfold it. "Well done!" it says. It is from Andrea and Rich. Their address is also there. I must remember to send them a postcard, and it has to be the one with the picture of the summit; the one Andrea looked at yesterday.

Outside the hut, there is still a big crowd gathered. Two people are carrying Brian up to the helicopter pad, and another one is talking through his intercom. The helicopter returns and lands only meters away from Brian. They lift him into the helicopter, the nurse jumps in behind him, and then it is gone.

I fly down in the other helicopter with the rescue guy from the mountain. It is almost dark, but despite that, we are not flying directly to Zermatt. The rescue team wants to use the opportunity to check the conditions on the Matterhorn's north wall. It is wildly fascinating: we are hovering about 50 meters from the mountain, swaying slightly from left to right. They have supplied me with a headset, but I do not understand what they are talking about.

Evening in Zermatt

'Look! It's Steffen!' shouts Phil, and promptly gives both Peter and Mark a slap.

'Hi guys...good to see you!'

'No, good to see you,' shouts Mark from his stool at the bar in The Brown Cow. He seems to have recovered completely.

The fact that I am probably a bit dehydrated from a long day on the mountain is not accepted as an excuse. Mark insists that beer is the only cure – and in large quantities, just to be on the safe side. It is an enthusiastic reception. They are sincerely happy to see me and immediately ask for Brian. I give them the short version.

Mark is running back and forth between our table and the bar.

'You must be hungry,' he says, and announces that he will go and ask the chef to prepare something for me.

'But...the kitchen closed hours ago, didn't it?' I ask.

'Yeah, and now they'll just have to open it again,' he responds and disappears off towards the kitchen.

These guys are just fantastic, and they want every detail. While I eat the best burger of my life, I tell them about climbing the Matterhorn: the big rock falls, the exhausted client, the other people we met, reaching the summit of course, the descent and the accident. My entire account is accompanied by constant supplies of beer.

'Hi guys!' salutes Brian as he enters the bar.

'Brian! It's so good to see you...come and sit down. No, let me help you...how are you? Damn, it's good to see you!' Mark cries as he slaps Brian on the shoulder with a force that almost sends him back out through the door.

Phil and Mark are shouting while Peter is trying to figure out how best to seat Brian.

In good spirits and with his leg in plaster, the patient is put through serious interrogation while the Irishmen order more beer. Brian describes how two friendly and understanding doctors took several X-rays to diagnose his problem: two serious fractures. They put his leg in plaster and gave him pills and injections to be taken daily to prevent blood clots. Had we not been acclimatized properly, this would probably not have been necessary; having set foot on the summit of the Matterhorn has resulted in an increase in the number of red blood cells and so an increased risk of blood clotting at sea level. Besides, with a fracture like Brian's, red as well as white blood cells will have enough work to do.

It is getting late and it has been a long and eventful day. All we need to do now is to get Brian safely through the village back to the campsite. We are looking forward to seeing our sleeping bags.

I cannot stop laughing. This is pure Jackass: the Irishmen have picked up a trolley from the railway station, and now they insist on driving Brian. Actually, he looks as if he would much prefer his crutches, but he has got no say in this. Normally, the main road seems wide enough, but now it is dangerously narrow. I fear the result will be another visit to the hospital. There is nothing I can do, though – every attempt to stop them is ruined by another outburst of laughter.

As Brian gets settled in the tent, I throw one last look at the Matterhorn, which rises as a shadow above the town. Just like yesterday and every other day.

The experiences from the mountain are racing through my head. This fantastic appealing mountain, which fascinates and frightens, does what it always does – it stands, unmoved and majestic. Tomorrow, other people will attempt to reach the summit. Some will hold their arms up high just as we did, celebrating reaching the summit of the Matterhorn. Before the year is over, about 5000 people will have tried. Of these, 10 to 20 will be dead.

Tired and worn, I search for my music player. Half awake, with a proud smile on my lips, I listen to Damien Rice and the song Cannonball, and I let it carry me off to sleep:

Stones taught me to fly
love taught me to lie
life, it taught me to die
so it's not hard to fall
when you float like a cannonball.
There's still a little bit of your song in my ear ...

Epilogue

As always, it was freezing cold in Rjukan, Norway. We were on our way along small, snow-covered tracks winding through the forest to the icefall at the bottom of the canyon. This is where we had decided to climb. Brian walked in front of me. He had not touched his climbing gear in seven months since he fractured his foot on the Matterhorn. In December, however, he announced that he was fit to join us on this year's ice climbing trip to Norway.

In the autumn that had passed, I had climbed in Sweden with Mads Andersen and Mugge. We had practiced the techniques and skills we would be needing during next summer's grand tour to Yosemite in California. We had big plans about big walls.

From time to time, I had called Brian to ask about his rehabilitation. During these conversations, I sensed that he was worried if the injury would leave him with permanent problems. We also talked about climbing; primarily about the experiences on the Matterhorn, but also about some of the old stories. We never talked about future trips, though. Brian did not say anything, and I did not want to pressure him.

'I don't know if I can still climb,' he said, as we approached the bottom of the valley. I knew that this was an issue. I had sensed his doubts already before we left. However, I had refrained from asking too many questions. I thought that this trip would give all the answers. I also knew that only Brian could make the decision.

Will you lead?' I asked when we were kitted up below the frozen waterfall. Brian nodded and slammed in his axes with great determination. First one, then the other. He placed them well. Then he pulled them out again and slammed them back in. He kept testing the placements and pulling the axes out again. Only one meter up, his legs were shaking badly. When you ice climb, lactic acid will often build up in your calf muscles, causing them to jitter like a jigsaw. This may result in the front points of your crampons losing their grip. Brian was not fighting lactic acid, however. He was afraid. He had to climb about five meters upwards before reaching a plateau, from which he could climb the main section of the ice-fall. Since he only needed to climb another meter or two, I encouraged him to go on.

Ten minutes later, we were both at the anchor just below the most difficult section. I had been convinced that I could climb it despite having the flu raging through my body. I could not, however; I was too weak. I asked Brian if he wanted to give it a go, but no.

'I can't, Steffen. I have lost it. I simply haven't got the guts to do it anymore. I'll have to stop climbing. This way it's too dangerous for both you and me. I can't focus on climbing and there is no joy. I keep thinking about all the things that might happen, and that I might fall and end up disabled. This is it, Steffen; I quit. I'll sell all my gear. You can have what you want, but the rest will go on auction tonight at the hut. I'm sorry, but I just can't.'

I looked at him. I was hanging three meters above him at an anchor point I had placed to relax my weak body.

'That's OK, Brian. I respect that.' We prepared an abseil and returned to the bottom. Half an hour later, we sat on our backpacks as we had done so many times before. The hot elderberry juice was steaming from our cups. We still had five hours before we would be picked up by the other climbers. I still wore my crampons. Brian removed his and put them behind him.

'It is so nice here, Steffen. Look!' said Brian and pointed towards the end of the valley where the winter sun had just conquered the clouds.

Glossary

Abseil:

A technique for lowering yourself on the rope using a belay device or figure-of-8.

Acclimatization:

A process through which you slowly enable the body to cope with altitude.

Alpine route:

A climbing route in the mountains with sections of ice and snow.

Altitude sickness:

A condition potentially caused by being at altitude when the body is not properly acclimatized.

Bergschrund:

A crevasse between the mountain wall and the glacier. The size of the bergschrund depends on the movement of the glacier and the steepness of the underlying terrain.

Bouldering:

In recent years, it has become increasingly popular to find and plan routes, so-called problems, on boulders. These 'problems' are close to the ground and are climbed without a rope.

Camming device:

Also: cam or cams and often called friends. A piece of climbing protection that, due to spring-loaded metal cams, can be placed in cracks of different sizes and with parallel sides.

Cornice:

An overhang of snow created by the wind and protruding from a ridge or mountain side.

Couloir:

A large gully on a mountain side prone to rockfalls and avalanches.

Crampons:

A set of metal points to mount under your mountain boots to get a better grip in snow and ice.

Crux:

The most difficult part of a climb.

Deadman:

A metal plate with attached wire for making an anchor in snow.

Dry tooling:

Using axes and crampons on rock (rather than on ice and snow).

Figure-of-8:

A piece of metal shaped like the figure '8'. Used as a friction device for abseiling.

Fixed equipment:

Pieces of equipment bolted to the rock on some routes.

Fixed rope:

Ropes permanently fixed to the rock on some routes.

Front pointing:

A technique which implies that only the front points of the crampons are in contact with the rock, ice or snow.

Gaiters:

Clothing to keep the snow out of your boots.

Gendarme:

A free-standing, rather large, rock steeple.

Munter Hitch:

A knot formed by winding the rope around a carabiner in a certain way. The knot acts as a two-way friction device. The person working the knot can hold another person's weight.

Ice screw:

A hollow metal screw with sharp teeth and an outside thread. A loop is placed on top for clipping to a carabiner.

Mixed climbing:

Climbing on a route with snow, ice and rock.

Moraine:

Gravel and rock pushed aside by the movement of a glacier.

Normal route:

Typically the easiest route on a mountain and often the one used on the first successful ascent.

Nut:

A cubic piece of aluminum threaded with a metal wire. Used as protection when placed in cracks in the rock.

Prusik:

A loop of thin rope. When the thinner piece of rope is tied in a certain way around a thicker rope, it locks when weight is put on it.

Quickdraw:

A short sling with a carabiner at both ends used to attach protection to the rope.

Running belay:

A time-saving technique that is often used on less difficult sections of a climb. Both climbers move simultaneously. The front climber places protection, which is removed by the second as he or she reaches it.

Sources

The sections in this book relating historical events are the result of my own research, through which I have found that there is not complete agreement in the literature about what happened when. Thus, my accounts may differ from those of others.

On several occasions, I mention certain numbers of climbers, deaths and rescue operations. These numbers are difficult to verify and are primarily based on interviews with the rescue service and mountain guides in Zermatt.

The First Ascent

- Exhibitions, conversations and different material from the Alpine Museum, Zermatt.

- Edward Whymper: Scrambles Amongst the Alps (National Geographic Books 2002)

- Eric Shipton: Mountain Conquest - Danish edition (Lademann 1968, Denmark).

- Beat P. Truffer: The History of the Matterhorn (Aroleit-Verlach 2001)

Altitude Sickness and Acclimatization

- Dr. Henrik Jessen Hansen: 'Om akklimatisering og højdesyge' (On Acclimatization and Altitude Sickness) in: Mont Blanc – oplevelser fra Europas top (Mont Blanc – Experiences from the Top of Europe) by Steffen Kjaer (Mellemgaard 2003, Denmark).

- Don Craydon, Steven M. Cox & Kris Fulsaas (eds.): Mountaineering – The Freedom of the Hills (Swan Hill Press 2003).

- James A Wilkerson (ed.): Medicine for Mountaineering (Mountaineers Books 2001).

- Portrait: The mountain guides Herbert Lüthi and Andreas Perren

- Interview in Zermatt

Poor Matterhorn

- Exhibitions, conversations and material from the Alpine Museum in Zermatt.

- Interviews with guides, rescue personnel and local Zermatt inhabitants.

Glaciers Shaped the Matterhorn

- Exhibitions, conversations and material from the Alpine Museum in Zermatt

President Roosevelt on the Matterhorn

- Alpine Museum in Zermatt

An Historic Evacuation

- Interview with pilot Fabian Zuber and mountain guide Andreas Perren

Winston Churchill

- Alpine Museum in Zermatt

- *The Matterhorn for Life*, by Nyle K. Walton, www.peakware.com

The Visitor's Book

- Copies of the Visitor's Book provided by The North Wall Bar in Zermatt. Some of the reports have been edited due to the sake of clarity.

Books and maps

Preparing for our climb, we read a number of articles and searched the Internet. We read accounts of previous climbs, but our primary support was found through local contacts and the following material:

Books

- Lindsay Griffin: Valais Alps West: Selected Climbs (Alpine Club 1998)

- Les Swindin and Peter Fleming: Valais Alps East: Selected Climbs (Alpine Club 1999)

- Richard Goedeke: The Alpine 4000m Peaks by the Classic Routes. A Guide for Mountaineers (Baton Wicks 2003).

Maps

- 2515 Zermatt – Cornergrat 1:25000.

Acknowledgements

First and foremost, it has been an exciting journey to write this book. Having the possibility to do so is a privilege in itself, and it has helped me re-live everything. Everywhere, I have met great interest in my project. I have been very happy with the helpfulness I have experienced, especially during my research in Zermatt.

David Gray

Two years ago, Brian gave me a CD by David Gray. I do not know why it has become my writing album number one; I just know that the keyboard felt differently, that the associations danced and the memories came trampling into my head when "White Latter" was playing.

Alpine Museum in Zermatt

I am indebted to the staff at the Alpine Museum in Zermatt, who took it upon them to open the museum outside regular opening hours.

Tourist Information in Zermatt

Before the first line of this book was ever written, I received great support from the Tourist Information in Zermatt. Both during my research and when I visited Zermatt, they helped me in very important ways.

The North Wall Bar

I was honored and humbled the day I left The North Wall Bar with the Visitor's Book, which the friendly owners allowed me to borrow and use in this book. What a demonstration of confidence!

Mugge (Mogens Dam)

When I returned to Zermatt, after having climbed the Matterhorn, to do research for this book, Mugge joined me. It was an exciting week during which the amount of laughs, amazing experiences and the interesting conversations we had with different people made a huge impression on me. I am so happy with the support I received from Mugge concerning this project, and with the enthusiasm he put forward in getting those good photos.

Herbert Lüthi and Andreas Perren

Through interviews with the mountain guides Herbert Lüthi and Andreas Perren, I got good insights in their everyday lives and really enjoyed their many stories. Thanks for trusting me.

Fabian Zuber

At Air Zermatt, I met the pilot Fabian Zuber, who told me about work at one of the busiest rescue services in the world. It was interesting, and, luckily, we were almost through with my questions when we had to stop the interview due to another emergency response.

Bruno Jelk and the Rescue Service

Naturally, I am grateful for the professional service supplied by pilots, doctors, nurses and Rescue Chief, Bruno Jelk, in relation to our accident. We never experienced any blame or annoyance, and the entire squad did a fantastic job. I really appreciate that.

Brian

At no point did I want to climb the Matterhorn with anyone else. If I forget your restless moments when the weather did not perform the way you wanted it to, and if I forget everything about your alternative expressions of joy when I over and over again asked you to take part in my numerous photo sessions, and if I remember my limited understanding of your highly developed norms, you have been a fantastic climbing partner.

We ventured out there to seek adventure. On trails and on mountain walls we learned something about ourselves, and everlasting traces were left in our souls. We shared the dream. Together we realized it. Thanks, Brian!